HISTORICALLY BLACK

I0112731

Historically Black

Imagining Community in a Black Historic District

Mieka Brand Polanco

NEW YORK UNIVERSITY PRESS

New York and London

NEW YORK UNIVERSITY PRESS
New York and London
www.nyupress.org

© 2014 by New York University
All rights reserved

References to Internet websites (URLs) were accurate at the time of writing.
Neither the author nor New York University Press is responsible for URLs that
may have expired or changed since the manuscript was prepared.

For Library of Congress Cataloging-in-Publication data,
please contact the Library of Congress.

ISBN: 978-0-8147-6288-2 (hardcover)
ISBN: 978-0-8147-6348-3 (paperback)

New York University Press books are printed on acid-free paper,
and their binding materials are chosen for strength and durability.
We strive to use environmentally responsible suppliers and materials
to the greatest extent possible in publishing our books.

Manufactured in the United States of America
10 9 8 7 6 5 4 3 2 1

Also available as an ebook

CONTENTS

ACKNOWLEDGMENTS

No book is ever written alone—and this project owes its existence to a large group of people. Each has contributed in small and great ways to the book, from its conception, through research and writing, over the process of reviews and revisions, and finally through to publication.

First and foremost my deep and sincere thank you to the residents of Union who have made this book a reality on every level: their generous hospitality gave me the opportunity to ask my many relentless questions; their insights, thoughts, and perspectives provided the seeds for much of the analysis I offer here; and their patient support afforded me the time and space to make sense of it all. I lament that for ethical and legal reasons your real names are concealed behind pseudonyms, but I would like to offer a heartfelt thanks to the residents I identify as Julia Peters, Jordan Lawson, Joanne Mitchell, and Louise Coles. I dedicate this book to the memory of Jim Gaines, Ernest Greene, Bill Anderson, and Celia Marshall who, sadly, passed on before the book was completed. Four unique people, they were sage, strong, stubborn, delightful human beings each in their own way. I have learned so much from each of you, and grown through our friendship.

I have been so fortunate to have a nurturing and supportive community of mentors, colleagues, and friends through the long gestation that yielded this book. These people have shaped my project—and me—in profound ways. Among these I am honored to include George Mentore, Hanan Sabea, Wende Marshall, Dell Upton, Charles and Nan Perdue, Edie Turner, Reginald Butler, Gertrude Fraser, T. S. Harvey, Nona Moskowitz, Sandy Alexandre, Candice Lowe, Tyron Simpson, Ethan Van Blue, Corey D. B. Walker, Patti Epps, Lisa Toccafondi Shutt, Jeane Siler, my beloved late friend

Ajit Serasundera, Makalé Faber, Yadira Perez Hazel, Eboni Bugg (and my fairy goddaughter, Sahara Clemons), Orly Rachmilovitz, Diarapha Diallo, Sevil Baltali Tirpan, Abigail Holeman, Asiya Malik, Carrie Heitman, Lisa Stewart, Anjana Mebane-Cruz, Melinda Reidinger, Michael Wesch, Davarian Baldwin, Cheryl Hicks, Megan Tracy, Christa Craven, and Raymond Gunn. A sincere thank you to the many people who have read, listened to, and commented on portions of this book, including my divinely patient editor, Jennifer Hammer, as well as Tim Sieber, John L. Jackson, Deborah Thomas, Dana-Ain Davis, and the anonymous reviewers who offered meticulous and poignant comments. You have each challenged my thinking, forced me to work and rework my arguments, refine the nuances of my analysis, and ultimately made this project far richer and more complex than I ever could have done on my own. Any shortcomings are, of course, mine alone. Thank you also to the financial and intellectual support of the Carter G. Woodson Institute for African-American and African Studies, and the University of Virginia's Department of Anthropology.

Finally, anyone who has embarked on a project as all consuming as writing a book can attest that the ultimate support is given—and sacrifice made—by one's own family. I cannot begin to capture how vital my amazing husband's encouragement and sustenance have been to seeing this project through. Omer and Eitan, our bright, beautiful boys, have brought sunshine into every one of my days since they came into my life. My courageous, talented mother, Gila Svirsky, has been my moral and intellectual role model, and an indefatigable and astute editor. My father, Shimon Brand's philosophical poise, wisdom, and thoughtfulness continue to awe and inspire me. Thank you to my late aunt, Sarah Schwartz, who helped me grasp the profound meaning of community. To my sisters, Denna Brand, Nira Brand, and Dorit Ely, and to Judy Kirshner, Ashlie Charlotte and Sheila Maité Polanco, Sally Gottesman, Suzanne Schwartz, Mercedes (Querida) Frias, Cynthia Mercedes, Genesis and Freddy Acosta, Melissa Roukous, Alexandra Teasdale, and Ashley Thompson: you have given me strength and perseverance to embark on—and complete—this journey. I thank you each from the bottom of my heart.

1

Introduction

In vain, great-hearted Kublai, shall I attempt to describe Zaira, city of high bastions. I could tell you how many steps make up the streets rising like stairways, and the degree of the arcades' curves, and what kind of zinc scales cover the roofs; but I already know this would be the same as telling you nothing. The city does not consist of this, but of relationships between the measurements of its space and the events of its past . . .
Italo Calvino, *Invisible Cities* (1974)

The town of Union[1] lies at the foot of the Blue Ridge Mountains in central Virginia. Before beginning my research there, I was given careful instructions to drive slowly as I approached the community. "It's so small and unassuming," I was told, "if you blink you'll miss it." The brick and wood-frame homes that make up Union are far enough apart that passersby see more trees and greenery than brick or mortar, but the houses that are visible from the road are a mixture of old and new. Dilapidated, century-old frame houses slowly decay into overgrowth beside carefully restored homes that sport trimmed hedges and long, private driveways, these standing beside newer prefabricated or cinderblock homes flanked by small vegetable gardens and work sheds. Union Road, the main artery through the community, is a two-lane country road that winds gently through the rolling hills before finally spilling into a heavily trafficked highway in a fast-growing and increasingly urban area.

To Union residents, these places are not empty of meaning. Indeed, each of the descriptions above—the homes, the winding road, the dilapidated frames—evokes memories, opinions, an emotional response. Although to an outsider Union may appear to be an unremarkable semi-rural community, like Calvino's Zaira it cannot be understood without a grasp of the interrelationship among residents, the space, and their collective history: the social relationships that produce—and are produced by—Union. To those who live and act in and around Union, the interrelationship among people, history and space transforms this place from a series of houses that could be missed by the blink of an eye into a distinct place: homes laid out in a particular pattern as a result of historical circumstances and creating a specific dynamic, a community shaped by intricate social relationships and events—experienced through the histories that residents narrate about these relationships and events.

In 1999 Union, Virginia, was federally recognized as a Historic District under the category "Ethnic Heritage—Black." To celebrate its recognition, the Union Community Association organized an unveiling ceremony for the historic highway marker. Since that recognition, Piedmont County officials began hailing Union as a "model community" and zoned it to prevent rapid new construction. Some residents adopted the official lingo, declaring with some pride that they live in a "historically black community." But while the term "community" seems to permeate every discussion about Union, it is far from clear what community means—and to whom. Does community refer to a group of people? To a physical landscape? To some combination of the two? While the term "community" might connote a cohesive social unit bound by a defined physical landscape, the reality differs significantly from this image.

Given the fact that Union has been home to a racially mixed population since at least the late 19th century, calling it "historically black" poses some curious existential questions to many of the black residents who currently live there. Union's identity as a "historically black community" encourages us to see this place as a monochromatic and monohistoric landscape, effectively erasing both old-timer white residents and newcomer black residents. This book examines the ways in which different groups of residents think and speak about "community" and how they map those ideas onto their homeplace. The result is a multilayered, multitextured ethnography of community, and an invitation to a public conversation about the dynamic ways in which race, space, and history inform our experiences and understanding of community. At its core this book offers an examination of the concept of community in the United States: how communities are experienced and understood, the complex relationship between human beings and their social and physical landscapes . . . and how the term is sometimes conjured to feign cohesiveness that may not actually exist. It argues that in the United States, race, space, and history form the scaffolding on which we construct our understanding of community. As a construct, community could potentially envelop endless combinations of racial identities, historical sensibilities, and relations to the physical landscape. And yet the term is more frequently used to gloss an oversimplified perspective of race, history, and space. Such a perspective conceals much of the richness (and contention) of lived reality in the United States both today and in the past, and allows Americans to avoid an important conversation about the complex and unfolding nature of community.

In the United States the deep entanglement of history, space, and race can be seen in practically every expression of the idea of community in daily interactions, popular culture, the evening news, and current academic scholarship.[2] Indeed, much of the vast body of literature that theorizes about the meanings and significances of community (see Delanty [2009] for a survey of this literature) frequently focuses on one or more of these three components—history, space or race—but only infrequently has the very intersection among all three been recognized as a meaning-ful point of departure for making sense of how community is shaped and experienced in this country today.[3]

Identifying Union as a "historically black community" not only casts an image of a monochromatic, monohistoric landscape, it also masks the fact that in this settlement neither racial identity nor historicity—nor even the physical boundaries of the community—are fixed. Instead, as was all too obvious in the unveiling ceremony for the Union historic highway marker, blackness is conflated with the past and fused to a spe-cific locale: black residents have become physical embodiments of history and thus confirm with their presence Union's status as both historical and black. Whiteness, on the other hand, escapes such definition, so while newcomer white residents are easily able to take on the role of preservers of history, old-timer white residents are rendered entirely invisible. Local productions of race, space, and history in Union are far richer than the official history lets on, and the voices of some residents are silenced at the very moment that their stories are told.

This book, then, is a quest to understand the inflections that race, space, and history have on people's experiences and understandings of community. This attempt to get at the three underpinnings of community is the result of fieldwork conducted in the small central Virginia town of Union. The goal of this work is not to disentangle space, history, or race as three separate categories but, on the contrary, to investigate how together they form a powerful triad shaping Americans' everyday experi-ences and understandings of community.

The data for this book were collected through ethnographic and archi-val fieldwork that I conducted in and around Union. During my time in the field, I learned from residents about their work, their lives, their histories, the things they consider important and the things they do not, how they think about their communities (and about the idea of commu-nity in general), and how they relate to the place they call home. Arriving on the scene just after Union gained official recognition as a Historic District, I had the opportunity to witness the disparate nature of people's experiences of community through the imbrication of race/space/history in their daily lives and how these experiences were reframed through the state's own definition of these terms. Each of the chapters that follows approaches this triad from a different angle, together creating a three-dimensional approach to the study of community as it unfolds in Union.

Introducing Union

As I drive along the old familiar road heading to Ms. Peters's house fourteen years after my first introduction to this town, I note how little has changed since the first time I visited the community. I wind around a curve on Union Road—the first one I would consider being in Union—and notice that the Nolans have already planted this year's corn. The new stalks are edging over the fence and I smile as I think of the still spry Ms. Nolan (though well into her eighties) excitedly recalling a long-ago trip to Graceland, or a visit with her beloved grandchildren. In a moment I pass by Mr. Gaines's home. He passed away a few years ago, but the old brick home still looks the same and even his trusted ride-lawnmower is still parked by the side entrance. Someone is living in the house . . . a grandson or nephew, I guess.

And there, on the left, is Mr. Lawson's beautifully restored home. An American flag gently waves over a white gravel driveway. I try to imagine what the house might have looked like when Mr. Lawson first bought it some 20 years ago. Already nearly a century old, the house had belonged to the Greenes, one of Union's old white families—and though they had been relatively secure financially, the careful attention that Mr. Lawson lavished on the house meant that the restored version was very likely far more elegant and grand than the original had ever been. No one is outside any of the houses I drive by. It is a work day—and, besides, people don't really spend time on the side of the homes facing Union Road. The traffic is too fast, and most neighbors prefer their side or backyards when they spend time outdoors.

At the community's single intersection, I'm surprised to see that the old church, Mt. Zion, is looking more rundown than I had ever seen it before. The white paint is peeling off the wide wood panels, and weeds have overtaken the narrow strip of grass that surrounds the building. It had been nearly ten years since the congregation outgrew the 100-seat sanctuary and began worshipping elsewhere, but as I take note of the decay—and the small "For Sale" sign beside the front doors—I wonder what Mr. Gaines would have said. I imagine him sending me a knowing look and smirk, as if to confirm his suspicion that the building would eventually be abandoned. In a moment I will arrive at Ms. Peters's small house, which for me marks the far end of Union, and I realize that to me, too, Union is an embodied set of relationships. From the moment I turned the first curve (a little too quickly, as usual), my body has been following its own familiar path through the community. My head turned—and my thoughts followed—in the same directions it always does. Over the years of traveling down this road and building relationships with some of the neighbors, I too have developed an embodied relationship to this place. My eyes fix on the same homes they always do—those that mean something to me—and I inadvertently gloss over those that do not. And what I see is not so much the physical materiality of the space, but the social relationships that the materials (and the spaces between them) signify.

Union does not easily lend itself to finite socio-geographic categories. It is a town to some, a neighborhood to others, a village or suburb to others still. It is historic according to the state and some of its residents. But it is also not historic to other residents and, in other contexts, also not historic to the state. To make matters more confusing, those who do consider Union to be historic generally agree that those residents who do not consider it historic are in fact the very link to Union's historic-ness. And despite these apparent contradictions, Union is not a place where definitions of history and space are being actively hashed out. Rather, most of Union's residents go about their daily lives with very little thought about its historic-ness (or lack thereof), and with very little contact among one another, coming together only at ritualized moments to communally celebrate what each believes Union to be: their neighborhood/village/town, a historic/not historic community. Union.

And so, I embark on the tricky task of laying before you Union, a place that (like many others) is borne by the interrelationship among history, space, and race, a place that seems to resist simple spatial and temporal categorization, and that became for me more elusive and less definable the more I came to know it.

Perhaps the most important event in bringing Union to local public attention was its official recognition by the National Register of Historic Places as a "historically black community." Each of the terms by which the NRHP's official narrative identifies Union—"historical," "black," and "community"—gives pause to those who know the community. Whether it is "historical" is up for debate. There is no question that Union has never been exclusively (or even predominantly) black, although African American residents have certainly lived in Union for perhaps two centuries. And the disparate lives of the residents challenge what is meant by "community." As I worked in Union, it was this very term, "historically black community," that led me to formulate the questions that lay at the center of my research: What makes Union "historical"? How (and by whom) was it defined as black? And in what way is the term "community" employed to describe (and ultimately experience) this place? Union was officially identified by the National Register of Historic Places (NRHP) as a Historic District under the category "Ethnic Heritage—Black." According to the NRHP nomination papers, Union was "founded by freed black slaves shortly after the Civil War." Two families in particular—the Marshalls and the Farradays—were identified as Union's founders, and the text notes that the settlement is still inhabited by some of their descendants. The nomination papers submitted to the NRHP portray Union as a place that encapsulates a moment in African American history, demonstrating not unusual or outstanding phenomena, but rather a presumably "typical" example of African-American experiences and lifeways in the region during the late 19th and early 20th centuries. Union, the nomination papers explain, is "one of the few remaining black communities established in [Piedmont County] after the Civil War."

Dilapidated home on Union Road. Photo by Larnell Flannagan.

A fairly lengthy history of Union, as recounted in the NRHP nomination papers, can be summarized as follows:

Union, Virginia, is located at the intersection of what had once been four slave-owning plantations. Some of the people who labored as slaves on these plantations did not reside on the plantation, but rather lived in houses outside the plantation. Legally, these tracts were owned by the nearby planters (federal law at this time prohibited enslaved people from owning property), but they were considered independent of the plantations themselves, and generally viewed as the homeplaces of the African American families who lived on them. In the late 19th century, after the Civil War ended and slavery was officially abandoned (in all cases except incarceration), four of the local African American families felt it was important to become the legal owners of their homes. Impoverished, these families could not buy the property outright, but were able to pool their resources and trade the labor of the men in the family for a deed to the land. Eventually, all four families were able to gain legal ownership of their land and homes.

A lot was changing in Virginia at the end of the 19th century, during the periods often identified as "post-bellum" and "Reconstruction." Black and white folks were moving around the Commonwealth (and the country) in an effort to cope with the new economic conditions that resulted from emancipation; people were reconfiguring their understanding of what race meant and the nature of their relationship to one another; and in the place about to be named Union, white merchants began living alongside the black residents. I have not heard anyone (or read anything) that describes this period in Union as harmonic or equitable, but the few commercial enterprises that opened in Union at this time (a post office, a dry goods store, a train station, and—for a short period—a mine) serviced all local residents. In 1871 Union's black residents once again banded together, this time to construct a church building to provide a permanent home for the congregation that had been holding services outdoors for many years. White residents established their own church, and in an ironic manner so typical of the American South, the tiny village of Union could be described as a segregated but thriving community.

Perhaps the most significant factors in Union's 20th century configuration were the advent of the car and the construction of a neighboring highway that led directly to the nearby town of Riverton. These two conditions portended Union's transformation from an independent, rural agricultural community to being part of a rural/suburban bedroom community. Gradually Union's commercial enterprises closed, and residents became increasingly reliant on Riverton for commerce, employment, and, when they could afford it, entertainment.

By 2000 (a year after historic recognition was conferred on Union), it was difficult to delineate where Union ended and the rest of greater Riverton began. The post office, which had been the catalyst for assigning Union a unique name (letter writers would need to identify a place name in the address), had long since closed, many residents (especially younger ones) moved away, and "Union" became primarily a reference to the road that cut through the town.

My work in Union began primarily as a result of its historical recognition. In 2000 I was hired as an intern by a local research institute to produce a public archive of materials related to Union's history. My task was to identify and compile materials from various archival sources (libraries, historical societies, governmental offices, and private collections), enhance these with a series of oral histories that I was to conduct with residents descending from the original founding families, and make them available to the public. Over the course of the summer I was able to collect more material than I could curate in one season, and we decided to extend the project for a second summer in 2001.

By this time a set of experiences hinted that a complex set of power relations was enfolded into Union's recognition as a historically black community, and into the entrenched role of history, space, and race in forming this community: I received a map of Union hand drawn by a white former resident and said to represent Union in the 1920s and 1930s; not even one black household appeared on the map. In an interview, a black resident told me that today Union no longer exists; "It used to be Union, but then the post office closed," he explained. "Now we're just Riverton." A newer (white) resident who was heavily involved in obtaining historical recognition told me that the official Union Historic District boundaries were based on the location of what the NRHP considered "contributing structures"—not on where residents historically considered Union to be. All of these experiences and others served as continual reminders that, like any living environment, Union was a dynamic place in which the meanings of history, space, and race were being actively negotiated, and correspondingly, that residents did not share a common vision of Union's status as a "historically black community."

And yet, not surprisingly, the NRHP nomination papers reveal none of this ambiguity, none of the richness I had experienced on the ground. "The [Union] Historic District," explain the NRHP nomination papers, "is significant under Criterion A as the best preserved and most thoroughly documented historically black community in the region." Beyond the bland language in a familiar bureaucratic tone there seemed to be hidden a far more complex tale that a federal document was unable to capture. Social geographer Edward Soja cautions, "We must be insistently aware of how space can be made to hide consequences from us, how relations of power and discipline are inscribed into the apparently innocent spatiality of social life, how human geographies become filled with politics and ideology" (1989:6). The time I spent in Union, and the interactions I had with its residents, all indicated that "relations of power" were hidden within Union's socio-geographic landscape, and I was eager to uncover them.

Early Fieldwork Experiences: Meeting Descendant Residents
Recording History

One of the first Union events in which I participated occurred in early May 2000. I was invited with two colleagues to meet with residents whom the NRHP had identified as descendants of the founding families. The meeting was organized by Regina Anderson, herself a descendant of the Marshall family and—I learned on the way to the meeting—a local historian as well. Ms. Anderson arranged for us to meet with three additional descendants—Julia Peters, Jim Gaines, and Margaret Adderly. The four ranged in age from 65 to 86, all were born in Union, and all had lived there for most or all of their lives; they each could trace their ancestry (usually about two generations back) directly to one of the families that the NRHP papers identify as Union's founders. As we arrived, Ms. Anderson shepherded us all—researchers and residents—into her living room where her husband, Bill, set out extra chairs to accommodate everyone. Once we were all present, Mr. Anderson disappeared into another part of the house and the rest of us took our places around a low coffee table stacked with old photo albums and memorabilia-filled shoeboxes.

"Thanks, everyone, for coming together," began my senior colleague. He placed a small tape recorder on the coffee table in front of him and turned it on. My second colleague did the same. "This is a great opportunity for us to officially record the history of the original African American families here in Union and to give them their duefully respectful position in terms of history." I sat quietly on the sofa, taking everything in. I was a young graduate student, and this was the first time I was meeting most of the people in the room. The truth is, I was feeling somewhat ill at ease. I had been brought in to act as a historian, but my training was in anthropology and I was still deciphering how those academic distinctions played out in real life. I knew that histories are always subjective, always told from a particular standpoint, and that they inherently leave out at least as much as they reveal.[4] Whatever I would choose to include in the archive, and however I organized the materials, would necessarily make a particular statement about Union's past, and I wanted to make sure that my work reflected the interests of these residents . . . as soon as I figured out what those interests were. As a historian I knew I would have to commit to one (subjective) historical standpoint. Naïvely, I assumed that I would also have to suspend my own interest in the politics of history and space, focusing instead on names, dates, places, chronologies—the kinds of "facts" I thought would be of interest to Union's residents, the research organization that hired me and future archive users.

As it turns out, my assumptions were wrong. Had I ignored the role historical narratives played in the lives of those with whom I worked, or the complex ways history was mapped onto Union, I would have missed a critical element of why Union's history matters in the first place—and to whom. I discovered that, like anywhere else, there was not one history of Union, but rather many histories that people narrated about the place. The nature of each narration—the places to which it referred, the particular facts it marshaled, the way it elucidated topics such as race and racism, and the role it played in residents' everyday lives and senses of identity—was shaped by the narrators' relationship to Union as a community.

I looked around at the four residents sitting in the room. They were listening attentively as my colleagues described the goals of the project.

Mr. Gaines, who was the oldest resident present, had his eyes fixed on the ground, nodding occasionally in response to the speaker's comments. The three women looked directly at the speakers, paying close attention to his every word. After a long preamble, the first colleague noted that he planned to make use of a video recorded by one of the newcomer neighbors a few years earlier. The neighbor's video was a recording of an interview he conducted with four descendant residents, including the three women sitting in the room this afternoon, Ms. Peters, Ms. Anderson, and Ms. Adderly.[5] Ms. Peters's opposition to our use of the video in the archive was polite, but immediate and unwavering.

> RESEARCHER: I have the copy of the videotape that, um, Ms. Peters and Margaret and Ms. Anderson . . . that you're all a part of.
>
> MS. PETERS: Hm . . .
>
> RESEARCHER: They're going to use that also as a part of this project.
>
> MS. ANDERSON: Oh, good.
>
> MS. PETERS: Oh, no. No! (pauses then laughs) We've got to talk about that.
>
> RESEARCHER: Well, no, no, no. They're going to pull some of the information. They're not going to use it. (laughs) They're just going to pull information from it.
>
> MS. PETERS: No. That's fine. (laughs politely) That was a disaster.
>
> RESEARCHER: But it was nice. Full of information.
>
> MS. ADDERLY: Yeah.
>
> RESEARCHER: And does he [the neighbor] have some other videotapes that he's done with you all also?
>
> MS. ADDERLY: No, no. We wanted to redo that one.
>
> MIEKA: We might be able to redo something.
>
> RESEARCHER: Right. But it has information, I think, that . . . (laughs), you know.
>
> MS. ANDERSON: . . . All those bouncing heads. (laughs)
>
> MIEKA: What's wrong with it?
>
> MS. ADDERLY: We just mainly talk about the pictures, I think.
>
> RESEARCHER: That thing with the dog, I guess.

MS. PETERS: The dog is—

RESEARCHER: (laughing) The dog is on there. The dog is barking.

MIEKA: Oh.

MS. PETERS: Also, somebody else is on the telephone, and somebody else is— (interrupted by researcher laughing) And the train. The train went by—

RESEARCHER: Yeah, the train went by. But still. The information is valuable.

My colleague, encouraged perhaps by Ms. Anderson's initial affirmative response ("oh, good"), brushes aside the concerns of Ms. Peters, who cites various interruptions that compromised in her opinion the value of the recording (a dog barking, someone speaking on the telephone, a train passing). In fact, she describes the recording as "a disaster." Her concerns were dismissed—but other concerns soon surfaced. This time it was Ms. Anderson who mentioned a master's thesis written about Union's architectural history. The author of the thesis had misidentified the name of one of the founders, incorrectly using the son's name (Zach Marshall) instead of that of the original founder (John Marshall). This mistake was amplified when the NRHP nomination papers repeated the error, incorrectly identifying Zach Marshall as one of Union's founders. Ms. Anderson explained that the mistake was corrected only because of her own persistent efforts. "The biggest problem with it [the thesis] is they're using the wrong Marshall," she notes. "It's Old Man John Marshall. Zach Marshall was one of his oldest sons. . . . See, I had a hard time trying to get them to change it, and finally they got to the point that they did. But it started out wrong."

Before any knowledge was exchanged, before the descendant residents chose to share with us "facts" about their past, they made sure we understood that they cared about history, cared about how they were being portrayed in an official historical narrative, and cared that their insights and opinions would be taken into consideration. While the researcher explained that the goal of the archive was to "really officially record the history of Union," the residents focused firmly on their concern over (mis)representation of their past in the historical narrative. They may not have been unanimous over which materials were appropriate for the official histories (Ms. Anderson approved the use of the video, while Ms. Peters did not), but their comments imply a shared concern with how Union's past should be made public, and an unequivocal desire that their insights be accurately represented.

It was important to Ms. Anderson that the correct name be attributed to Union's founder, and she relates her efforts to amend the careless mistakes that were made—and repeated—by outsiders. Ms. Peters was reluctant to have us use the videotape because much of what was said was muffled by dog barks, phone conversations, and a passing train. Although she laughs politely at the researcher's off-hand dismissal of her objection, she never backs off from her request. "No," she insists. "That's fine" (which, with her intonation, implies "we can do without that"). As I learned with time, the four residents in the room shared a sense of community that was based on memories directly linked to the place they knew as Union. They recognized that history is shaped by the standpoint of its narrators, and wanted official histories of Union to represent the standpoint they collectively held.

Fellowship: History as a Catalyst for Sociality

As soon as the formal part of our meeting ended and the tape recorders were turned off, the social dynamic in the room changed tangibly. From historical subjects, the descendant residents became our collective hosts, and we transformed from researchers to guests. Our initial roles (researchers/subjects) did not, of course, dissipate entirely, but in the new setting our interactions were determined primarily by our host/guest relationship. While in the first part of the meeting the researchers guided the flow and topic of conversation, in the reconfigured setting it was now the hosts who were setting the tone. Ms. Anderson invited us all to the dining room where she had set out a tasty array of food: chicken wings, macaroni and cheese, potato salad, vegetable salad, greens, bread, desserts, and drinks. . . . We filled up our plates as Ms. Anderson turned on the television. To my surprise, she began playing the very video that Ms. Peters had contested earlier. Also to my surprise, Ms. Peters, who earlier was adamant about not wanting us to use the video in the research project, now seemed perfectly content to have us watch it in our capacity as guests.

The room was a little raucous while we watched, and the quality of the sound emanating from the old television was poor. Friendly conversation flew back and forth between the dining room and living room, mixing compliments for the food with memories of the past, and interlacing comments with those that came from the television set: "That's Ms. Celia Marshall there, sitting next to me. She lives right down the road." "Oh, there goes that dog. That thing was so loud you can't hear a thing we say." Laughter and conversation followed each comment, with people talking over the videotaped voices, debating which historical family member lived in which now dilapidated house, sharing memories of a chimney that collapsed over the past winter, and returning to the screen to pick up another strand of videotaped history for more conversation.

Between the din in the room and the disruptions in the recording I did not catch much of what was said on screen. But I gathered fairly quickly that in the new setting—in our roles of hosts and guests—the specifics of what was said in the videotape were not as important as the opportunity that the recording gave us for fellowship. It allowed us to relate in a pleasant and informal manner, to transcend our obvious and less obvious differences and affirm similarities and mutually shared beliefs. While the video was arguably inappropriate as research material, it seemed to be entirely appropriate as an impetus for fellowship, for engaging each other sociably.

Mss. Anderson, Peters, and Adderly and Mr. Gaines have all known each other since their early childhoods. As I became more involved in the community and came to know these and other residents, I learned that they grew up in close proximity to one another and share many rich memories. The act of history telling (and history viewing, as with the videotape) provided them with occasion to reminisce, affirm ties of friendship and kinship, and connect their memories to the land, to their home-place, and to their own pasts. As hosts, these descendant residents could also draw their guests into the experience, sharing their memories and insights and inviting us to see Union through their eyes. This was an approach to history markedly different from the one my historian colleagues had offered earlier in the afternoon. In the earlier exchanges, history telling (or "harvesting" as the academics sometimes called it) was envisioned as an exchange between two opposed groups: subjects and researchers, those who "owned" history—and those who were there to "collect" it. "Truth" and "accuracy" were recurrent themes in the earlier conversation. Now as hosts and guests, history telling had unexpectedly revealed itself as a catalyst for sociality.

I wish that I could remember all that was exchanged that afternoon after the tape recorders were shut off, but at the time I did not think to commit these interactions to writing or memory. I recall that our hosts were curious to learn about us, where we came from, and how each of us had become involved in the project. I remember a charming and warm response from Ms. Adderly and Ms. Peters when I said I was from Israel, and a short conversation followed about growing up in the Middle East, violence, politics, and religion. By a good meal and comfortable conversation, we took the first steps towards getting to know each other. It was still many months before meaningful, long-term relationships were established, but in some small way we began to build a foundation through these four residents' gracious hospitality.

The Union Community Association Annual Picnic

A second event during this same summer took my research in Union on an unexpected turn, complicating my understanding of the residents' relationship to history and space, and who the subjects of my research should be. This second event took place at the opposite end of summer, as I was wrapping up the data-collection phase of my internship and beginning to organize the materials I had amassed—interviews, legal documents, letters, photos—into organized files. Sometime in late September I was invited by the Union Community Association (UCA) to attend an annual picnic for the residents of Union. Although I had not heard of the Association until the invitation arrived, a colleague from the research institute reported that its members were excited to have a "partner in their efforts" to record Union's history. They had been keen on getting this history recorded and glad to find that the institute I represented shared their interest. The picnic would be casual, we were told, but the UCA requested that the researchers say a few words there about our findings. We happily obliged.

On the day of the picnic, I drove to the address on the invitation and found myself in the driveway of a beautifully restored old brick home surrounded by expansive, well-groomed grounds. The house was unlike any of those I had visited over the summer. The homes of descendant residents were well kept, but by comparison simple and run-down. Although their construction was more recent than this house where the picnic was being held (most were built in the 1940s and 1950s), continual use revealed the half-century of wear and tear. In contrast, the house where the picnic was held was a 19th-century construction, but had been renovated and restored so that, even though it was well over a hundred years old, its original grandeur became an urbane backdrop to new amenities and appliances, posh grounds, and all the comforts of a new home.

I had spent the summer getting to know Union's African American residents, but as I joined the picnicking group, I found an equal number of black and white attendees, and many more people than I had expected. I was glad to see the familiar faces of the descendant residents I became acquainted with over the summer, and wondered who the rest of these people were. To my surprise, many somehow seemed to know me. People walked up and introduced themselves: "Mieka, it's nice to finally meet you! How is the archive project coming along? We can't wait to see it. Have you interviewed Mr. Gaines yet? He's a wealth of knowledge. Here, come meet Mr. Eagan, his family has been living here since the 1700s . . ."

Who were all these people?

"Important History"

When the picnic attendees reached a critical mass, Michael Taps, a white resident and (I soon learned) president of the Union Community Association, beckoned everyone to gather around him—perhaps 50 of us in all. Mr. Taps announced the events for the afternoon: we would begin with an opening prayer led by Mr. Jim Gaines; continue with brief words by UCA vice president Jordan Lawson; hear an update on the archiving project from the researchers; and conclude with a blessing for the food led by Mr. William Anderson. After these events, we could get on with the main activities of the afternoon—eating and mingling.

Jordan Lawson's speech was short, but highlights especially well some of the fundamental characteristics of the group of residents I eventually came to think of as Union's history brokers. He began by thanking our host for opening his home to the Union community—a white man with a cheerful smile responded by waving his hand and thanking all the guests for coming. Lawson continued with an announcement that the UCA had elected Ms. Julia Peters as Union's "person of the year," admitting that the choice was an easy one—Ms. Peters's ongoing contributions to the Association and the Union community at large made her an obvious and unanimous vote. Ms. Peters was surprised and embarrassed to receive the award ("I was shocked!" she later told me, smiling). I knew from our meetings over the summer that she generally prefers to stay out of the spotlight, but she was also visibly delighted when 50 pairs of hands applauded as she accepted her title and gift.

In conclusion, Jordan Lawson remarked that he was especially pleased to be joined by representatives from the research institute. As we all know, he summarized, Union is a historically black community founded in the 19th century, and people like Mr. Gaines and Ms. Adderly, who descend from the original founders, remember a lot of its history. The UCA were proud, he reported, of their success in achieving official historic status for Union—but the work was not over. Official recognition was a first step towards protecting Union's history. The project of writing a more complete history of Union still needed to be done. On behalf of the Community Association, Mr. Lawson commended the researchers for taking on the project, amassing an archive for Union and recording oral histories. He then turned to me directly and said that he hoped that after the summer project was over I would consider making Union the subject of my dissertation research. Lawson said he felt Union has an important history and an interesting story to be told, and he expressed his hope that I would help tell it.

I knew that my job as an intern was to be a historian, but my experiences and interactions with Union's descendant residents over the summer, and the new light in which they were now cast, tugged at my anthropological sensibilities. According to the NRHP nomination papers, Union is a "historically black community." I had spent the summer getting to know residents and collecting historical materials that fit into my notion of what the terms "historic," "black," and "community" meant. It did not occur to me to question whose terms these were or how they were intended, but the picnic—and especially Jordan Lawson's speech—made me wonder. If this is an African American community, then what were white folks doing at the picnic? It seemed that the Community Association was responsible for historic recognition, and even for initiating the archive I was working on. Who were its members? Whose standards were used to determine whether Union's history is "interesting" or "important"? What were the social dynamics among Union's various residents?

On one level Mr. Lawson's words had a familiar timbre. I recognized the same tenderness in his references to Union's past that I heard in my interviews with the descendant residents. Mr. Lawson described Union as having once been a small, cohesive community, a description I heard many times in my conversations with descendant residents—and the atmosphere at the picnic made me wonder whether this might not still be an appropriate description. But his words also had another quality that was entirely new—foreign, even. I had never heard any of the descendant residents I interviewed describe Union's history as "important." On the contrary, my interlocutors frequently hedged their accounts by explaining that their experiences were not historic—not outstanding or significantly different from what other people in the area were doing at the time. In our discussions descendant residents certainly related memorable and unusual experiences, but these were framed as idiosyncratic personal memories, not memories that had meaning beyond what they meant to them individually. When descendants couched their narratives within larger historical processes (e.g., Ms. Adderly told me about when her husband was in the Korean War), they did so in order to contextualize personal experiences, not to make claims of their importance, nor as anecdotes about larger historical processes (for example, Ms. Adderly never framed her husband's military experience as representative of some larger aspect of the Korean War).

In contrast, Jordan Lawson claimed that Union's history was "important." Speaking on behalf of the Community Association, he attested that they were "proud" of their success in gaining official historic status for Union and eager to make Union's history public. Although he did not articulate precisely what about Union's past he considered important (was it merely the presence of African American residents in Union during the 19th century? were any people or events particularly significant? does the presence of descendant residents living in Union today contribute to this "importance"?), Mr. Lawson stated unequivocally that recording Union's history was needed and promised that it would even make an interesting story.

As I learned over the course of my subsequent research, Mr. Lawson's speech at the annual Union picnic articulated some of the prominent features of the group I identify as "history brokers." Three elements in particular characterize Union's history brokers—which include, among others, the Union Community Association officers, the videographer of the aforementioned videotape, and (to some extent) the cheerful host of the picnic—and distinguish them from the descendant residents. These elements are (1) their racial and geographical identities, (2) their relationship to Union's history, and (3) their understanding of Union as a community.

Dramatis Personae

In all there are approximately 55 houses within the boundaries of the Union Historic District that are currently occupied and perhaps a dozen more that stand empty and are in various states of disrepair. As one drives along Union Road, it is easy to overlook the uninhabited houses: once abandoned, the old wood structures are soon consumed by the brush and almost indistinguishable from the surrounding greenery. Among the homes that are occupied, this book concentrates on those residents who are actively engaged in the process of history making, either as narrators ("history brokers") or historical subjects ("descendent residents"), or those who uncomfortably straddle the roles of narrator and subject—but are mostly ignored in mainstream historical narratives ("delegitimized historians").

Among the residents on whom this research pivots, there are six or seven families that I identify as "history brokers" (three with whom I conducted most of my research). There are some fifteen households that I call "descendent residents" (seven of whom were the focus of my research) and five to ten families that can be described as "delegitimized historians" (three with whom I conducted research).[6] For me, this last group was the most difficult to capture because they were fairly invisible in the channels that led me to Union in the first place, and because they themselves were mostly averse to the kind of research I was conducting. There may have been additional families in Union that I would have considered delegitimized historians, but since I did not cross paths with them during my fieldwork and was never introduced to them by other residents, I simply do not know about them.

History Brokers

Of the 55 (or so) households in Union, about 30 are inhabited by new-comers, and six or seven of these comprise the group I am calling "history brokers." At the most basic level, Union's history brokers are decidedly non-descendant residents both from their own perspective and from that of descendants themselves—but they were the pivotal actors in gaining recognition for Union as a Historic District. Geographically, history brokers are not native to Union, and they are white—two factors that mark them as distinctly non-descendants. These factors determine the history brokers' relationship to Union, its history and residents, and they also determine the placement of the history brokers within Union's social structure.

As white non-natives, Union's history brokers perceive themselves (and are perceived by others) as belonging to a different cultural unit from descendant residents. This distinction is reflected not so much in actual differences of cultural practices as in the fact that they are practiced separately. While similarities between the social practices of Union's various residents certainly exist, residents' day-to-day lives are mostly separate. History brokers and descendant residents come together on some occasions (such as the annual picnic) and are, indeed, pleased when they have the opportunity to present a public image of a united "interracial" (possibly even "post-racial") community. But such occurrences are rare, and the image reflects an ideology of a racially integrated society more than it does an everyday, lived reality in Union. Outside the annual picnic and occasional UCA meetings (which themselves are hardly attended by descendant residents), history brokers and descendant residents lead mostly separate lives.

As I conducted fieldwork I learned that Jordan Lawson, like other history brokers, had moved to Union as an adult. For residents such as Lawson, the choice to make a home in Union was based on quality of life and proximity to job opportunities. Union is near enough to the city of Riverton to make for a reasonable commute to a variety of employment opportunities, but far enough to allow residents to enjoy the spaciousness, serenity, and charm of "country living" in Union. Though history brokers each moved to Union from separate places, their social status as non-natives of Union is shared.

Living in Union was an active choice history brokers made, and while some have been living there for more than two decades, they are perceived (and perceive themselves) as permanent outsiders. Given this status, it is interesting that Jordan Lawson and his family, like our picnic host, the videographer, and many of the residents I am calling history brokers, chose to move into old houses they have renovated and updated, while retaining an aura of aged elegance. This choice hints at a relationship to the past that is expressed by brokers in other contexts as well. The aged aura of these renovated houses is an aesthetic, a "patina" (to invoke anthropologist Arjun Appadurai's term) that indexes character or even aristocracy. "The aura here is old, but the improvements are pragmatic and up-to-date," reads a local newspaper ad for a house for sale on Union Road.

The proper aging of things—houses, historical artifacts used to decorate the house, even stories about original inhabitants (mostly white families whose children have grown up and moved away)—is carefully managed so that their character and elegance is passed on, but only after a proper "dusting." "Patina is a slippery property of material life, ever open to faking as well as to crude handling," writes Appadurai (1996:75). But contrary to the English country house that Appadurai describes, patina in Union is achieved not through the appearance of "temporal continuity undisturbed," but precisely through a disturbed temporal continuity. It is not one's own old things that produce "the subtle shift of patina from the object to its owner," but the ability to acquire old things; not to inherit, but to come to possess them. The labor (and expense) required for becoming the owner of old things is what Union's history brokers value. And the indexing of this investment is what distinguishes "the successful semiotic management of the social context" (1996:76). By skillfully positioning old things so that they punctuate a modern décor, by making history a time-tempered accessory that complements the new (and not the other way around), Union's history brokers successfully manage to embody the patina of the old things they now own.

The second element distinguishing Union's history brokers is that they invest energy into bestowing honor upon descendant residents. Honor is a value produced through a dialectic between social persons and society at large. As noted by social anthropologist J. G. Peristiany, honor (and its counterpart, shame) is "the reflection of the social personality in the mirror of social ideals" (1966:9). Bestowing honor, as part of the dialectic, is a way for society—or, more specifically, for the state on behalf of society—to affirm the social behavior of certain citizens as honor worthy. "Every political authority," writes British anthropologist Julian Pitt-Rivers, "displays the pretention to incarnate the moral values of the society which it governs, to 'command what is right and prohibit what is wrong'; it therefore claims the right to bestow 'honours' and it follows that those whom it honours are, so it maintains, honourable" (1966:22). As we will see, in bestowing honor on descendant residents, Union's history brokers take upon themselves the role of representing an otherwise rather amorphous "political authority"—the National Register of Historic Places. By recognizing their honor-worthy neighbors—and virtual subjects—history brokers simultaneously assert themselves as intermediaries between descendant residents and the state, as official spokespersons on behalf of descendants, narrating their history and at the same time sanctioning the narrative. It is through this very role, I argue, that these residents—perhaps six or seven households in all—become the brokers of history.

Finally, and perhaps obviously given the first two elements, history brokers are residents who relate to Union's history as narrators, but not historical subjects themselves. This element harks back to the contrast, noted above, between what descendant residents consider to be personal memories, but which Jordan Lawson describes as "important history." Lawson, and Union's history brokers in general, approach history as a macro-level narrative in which the stories of descendant residents are case studies and anecdotes. History brokers believe that Union's history is "important" and "interesting," and they are committed to making it public—but they themselves do not figure into the narrative. Even though they are residents of Union, history brokers are markedly not descendant residents—they are not native, not black, not members of the same social circles. History brokers encourage descendant residents to contribute their memories and experiences to the official history, but as perpetual outsiders they themselves are never part of the narrative. Instead, they act as conduits for the descendants' narratives, molding them into what they believe "history" should look like.

History brokers are interested in garnering a public audience for descendant residents' history. This role is central to understanding history brokers' relationship to history and space, and for discerning some of the social and political dynamics that emerge from Union's official recognition as a historically black community. What most distinguishes Union's history brokers as a group is the role they take as intermediaries between the descendant residents (as vessels of history) and the world at large (who may be interested in learning about this particular history). As brokers, these residents are engaged in making Union's history available and palpable to a broad audience beginning with the NRHP (in the nomination papers for official historic status), continuing with visitors to the archive we researchers produced, with the hope of eventually reaching an ever greater audience through a yet-to-be-written public history. In producing a public history of Union, history brokers are not so much commodifying the past as offering the service of connecting those who "own" history with those who are interested in it.

Union's history brokers might feel that in some ways history is Union's very essence. To them, histories—narratives about the Union's past—are not primarily a vehicle for sociality (though sociality is by no means discouraged). Neither can histories be summarized as a mere recording of facts (though they would agree that creating records is a key element in the history-making process). Rather, to history brokers, Union is itself both the site of historical processes (containing the pasts of people and events that made Union) and the recording of these processes (the old buildings still standing in Union and the descendant residents living there are perceived as a sort of record of the past). Union's history brokers believe that the past should be preserved, recorded, honored, and celebrated, and they make an effort to ensure that this happens.

"Welcome to Union," UCA president addressed the audience at the unveiling ceremony for a historic highway marker, "a community. Not a road." Even though some history brokers have been living in Union for over two decades, and although many consider each other friends, the group I identify as history brokers is not necessarily one that its members themselves recognize. Union's history brokers socialize with one another and consult each other on issues, including the historical nomination or the annual picnics, but they tend to think of themselves not as a distinct social unit but as appendices or outsiders to more "authentic" Union-ites. This is in part because compared to Union's descendant residents, they share only a brief past together.

As transplants, Union's history brokers each have a unique past, a path not common to other residents: some hail from nearby Virginia communities, while others are transplants from more distant places in the country. Many work in the nearby city of Riverton, some in governmental positions or private sector, white-collar jobs. Of the three groups discussed in this book, that of the history brokers is the least organic— mainly because they imagine themselves as somewhat inauthentic members of the community; but the resident history brokers are also the most committed to the idea (and indeed the existence) of the larger social unit, the "Union community."

Descendant Residents

The labels "descendant residents" and "history brokers" are both based on the groups' relationship to history, but the nature of this relationship is distinct in each group. While "history brokers" refers to how that group approaches the narration of history, "descendant residents"describes how these residents fit into the narrative: history brokers are united by their shared desire to record Union's (black) history, while descendant residents get swept into the narrative regardless of what they happen to think about it, simply because of their genealogical ties to certain 19th-century historical actors.

The group I identify as "descendant residents" includes approximately 15 families whose members were born and raised in Union, and who have lived there for most or all of their lives. Many of the residents with whom I spent the majority of my time in Union were relatively elderly, though I also spent time with their offspring—children, grandchildren, and great-grandchildren—some of whom have moved away from Union, but who return to visit regularly. The age of most descendant residents (at least over 60 in 2001) meant that they were raised and educated at a time when racial segregation was practiced both de facto and de jure—and their attitudes towards history were to a large extent framed by these experiences.

The residents I identify as descendants are by definition African American, since they descend from Union's founders whom the NRHP nomination papers define as "former black slaves." They are also all second-generation residents of Union at least, even though the NRHP papers did not identify all of their ancestors as founders. I include all second-generation (or later) black residents as descendants because doing so allows me to capture an organic social unit that its members themselves would recognize. Since not all ancestors of these residents were identified in the NRHP papers as founders, my definition of descendant residents gives precedence to residents' own lived experience instead of the historical narrative recorded in the NRHP nomination papers—papers that (even the authors acknowledged) were authored by non-descendants and worded to fit NRHP expectations and guidelines.

Compared to history brokers, whom I define by what they are not (not native, not descendants, etc.), descendant residents are a much more coherent group. Their shared past and close interactions with one another mean that they also tend to share similar experiences and values, including similar attitudes towards the idea of "community" and the ways history and space shape this term. The particular racial climate in which many of the descendant residents were raised (particularly those born in the 1950s or earlier) was marked by social and legal segregation during the Jim Crow era, and by racism that continues on many social levels even today. As a result, descendant residents, who share the racial designation "black," cohere as a social unit through shared experiences and being bound into the same social spaces.

The oldest of these residents, Ms. Celie, remembers the small two-room schoolhouse, the "Union School," which African American children could attend for a short period during the 1910s. Around 1920 the Union School was closed. Parents were told that the state could not justify the school's upkeep (salaries for two teachers, a wood stove stocked and maintained by the children themselves, and no electricity) given the small number of students—even though the other "Union school," Union's white schoolhouse, which served fewer students, was kept open. After the schoolhouse closed its doors, parents sent school-aged children first to another nearby "colored school" that was run privately by a black Baptist church, later to a training school where they were taught "domestic sciences" and "vocational agriculture,"[7] and by 1951 to a somewhat more liberal arts–oriented but still segregated countywide school. All these institutions were segregated, designated specifically for African American students, all required some effort to attend (many were a significant commute away—especially at a time when roads were less reliable and private cars far less common than today), and all were focused primarily on what was called "manual labor" training.

Union's descendant residents did not have access to the kind of education that their white neighbors did, but, like anyone, they did the best with what little they had. Several of the descendant residents had lifelong careers in nursing, one of the few jobs open to black citizens that offered some degree of development and advancement. Others went off to the army or the Civilian Conservation Corps,[8] serving in (and between) every armed conflict from the Second World War to the wars in Afghanistan and Iraq. Others still worked as domestics in private households, as barbers, plumbers, and farm and railroad laborers—jobs that were available to African Americans, and for which they had already received training in school. To make money stretch (and partly as a legacy passed down from their parents), descendant residents supplemented the food they could buy with homegrown vegetables and home-raised hogs, goats, and cattle. And though most residents no longer keep livestock, almost all still grow their own vegetables even if they no longer rely on them as a main source for fresh produce.

Inasmuch as history brokers poured energy into honoring the descendant residents, descendant residents for their part accepted the gestures, though they did not demand or even expect them. Ms. Anderson, the woman who had hosted my colleagues and me in the gathering described above, served as the community's local historian, keeping records about people and events around Union. When history brokers initiated the process of gaining NRHP recognition of Union as a Historic District, Ms. Anderson was a willing collaborator. She contributed documents and stories, and encouraged others to do the same. For a short while, there was a flurry of interest in the pending publicity of Union's history. However, this interest was short lived. Fairly soon after NRHP officially recognized Union as a Historic District and the various ceremonies were over, descendants returned to their normal lives without much attention to the honors they were given by history brokers—nor were they resentful about a process that straddled a delicate balance between honoring and patronizing them.

According to Pitt-Rivers (1968), honor has three facets: it is a feeling, a behavior, and a treatment in response to this behavior. "The facets of honor may be viewed as related in the following way," he writes: "honor felt becomes honor claimed. And honor claimed becomes honor paid" (1968:503). Oddly, in the relationship between Union's history brokers and descendant residents, the third facet of honor (honor paid) preceded the first two facets (honor felt and honor claimed). In other words, Union's descendant residents were paid honor for their "historic-ness" without themselves having felt or claimed honor in terms of historic-ness. We saw earlier that honor is borne in a dialectic between social persons and society at large. In Union this dialectic produced a reverse relationship among Pitt-Rivers's three facets of honor: in Union history brokers paid honor to descendant residents, which eventually became honor claimed by descendant residents. And honor claimed became—for a short while, at any rate—honor that some of the descendants also felt.

As we will see, descendant residents and history brokers do not share the same sense of what constitutes honor-worthy behavior. Because history brokers consider history to be itself a quality worthy of honor, they pay respect to descendants who are viewed as "historical." But the premise of the honor paid by history brokers was not shared by descendant residents. Descendant residents, for their part, feel and claim honor in terms that are meaningful to them. Two major facets through which descendants tend to feel and claim honor are what they perceive to be an appropriate relationship to labor and religion. It is significant that descendants' sense of honor is produced through labor and religion, since both depend on acts over which descendants themselves have immediate control. One's relationship to the past (that is, from whom one descended and what that historical actor may have done) is predetermined and has nothing to do with one's own works and accomplishments. The quality of one's labor, on the other hand, and the depth of one's spiritual faith, are just the opposite: they are entirely contingent upon one's own choices and actions and, at least for Union's descendant residents, much more meaningful in how honor is understood and when it is felt, claimed, and perceived.

The homes of descendant residents, for example, demonstrate a particular relationship to history and the past. Though their houses are old, they do not attempt to "patina-ize" them or the surrounding landscape. Those "old things" in their homesteads that were remnants of the past— the gardens, the old sheds or vehicles some had on their property— indexed to descendants a particular and personal past: it was *Aunt Rose's* old house, the garden was planted by *my husband,* or this was *our* old car. Unlike history brokers' homes, "old things" in the homes of descendant residents signified not a generic past-ness but specific social relationships. More frequently, "old things" were around because they were actually being used or were never thrown away. The old tractor-mower that could have been displayed as a quaint curiosity on the lawn of a history broker's home was parked behind the home of a descendant resident because it was still being used to cut his lawn. A heavy iron skillet sits on the stove in the home of a descendant family rather than hanging on the wall as it might in the home of a history broker. It is precisely the "temporal continuity undisturbed," to return to Appadurai (1996:76), that denies these items the patina they might have acquired in the home of a non-native history broker.

There was no attempt by descendant residents to manage perceptions of the temporality of one's home, to emphasize its age, to preserve old features, or to glorify its past. Appadurai notes that patina embodies the "anguish of those who can legitimately bemoan the loss of a way of life" (1996:76). In Union, it is the privilege to disconnect from the past, from a way of life, that allowed things and people to acquire patina. History brokers had access to this privilege. Descendant residents did not. "People say 'the good old days,'" Mr. Gaines used to tell me. "They weren't no 'good old days' to me. No thanks. You can keep 'em."

Delegitimized Historians

In the field, identifying descendant residents and history brokers was a fairly easy affair. I recognized the descendant residents because I had already been introduced to many of them during my first summer of fieldwork in 2000. I recognized history brokers through our interactions at the picnic—they were the attendees who appeared to be orchestrating the events, or who expressed a desire to publish a history of Union. But there was another, third group of residents living in Union—some also present at the picnic—whom I did not at first recognize, but who ended up playing an important role in my research. These were Union's delegitimized historians.

Structurally, Union's delegitimized historians fit into a similar place as descendant residents. Like the descendants, they were born and raised in Union, and are second- (or more) generation residents. Like the descendants also, they were educated in segregated schools, and those who were old enough to have been schooled in the 1920s had attended a small schoolhouse in Union itself—also named the "Union school." Delegitimized historians, too, grew up in households where vegetables were grown and hogs and cattle raised as the household's main source of food. But delegitimized historians had very little day-to-day contact with the descendant residents, and their families are not listed among Union's founders in the NRHP nomination papers. This is because, in contrast with descendant residents, delegitimized historians are white.

The nomination papers for the National Register of Historic Places mention white residents living in Union as early as the mid-18th century, but in these papers they are not identified as founders, and the details of their presence are vague. For example, a section describing Union during the Reconstruction Period (1865–1891) describes the plots and family makeup of the "founding families," and notes that "the [1870] census lists a number of black families from whom several of [Union]'s current residents descend." There is no mention in this section that the census also lists an equivalent number of white families in the same tract, whose residences are interspersed with those of the black families.

To be sure, the NRHP narrative was written with the explicit purpose of highlighting Union's black history. The NRHP requires that applicants choose a category under which their potentially historic site will be recognized. The authors of Union's nomination papers (under the direction of Union's history brokers) chose the category "Ethnic Heritage—Black." The text in the nomination papers reflected this choice in order to support the argument that Union is sufficiently historic and sufficiently black to qualify for official historical recognition. "Sufficiency" here is somewhat ephemeral because, although the NRHP offers some guidelines for how to determine whether a site is eligible to apply for historic recognition, it is ultimately up to NRHP reviewers to determine whether a site (or, more accurately, an application) has "hit the mark." Cognizant of this process, the authors of the Union application took care to construct a historical narrative amenable to the NRHP criteria. To do so, white residents had to be marginalized for the central narrative. Too much attention to white residents would take away from the strength of the application as representative of black history, and so Union's racially mixed demographics were glossed over in favor of a simplified narrative about the "black community" in Union.

But marginalizing white residents in the nomination papers was not a strategic ploy used to dupe the NRHP. It was, in fact, reflective of a social reality practiced by the residents themselves. Life in Virginia between the 1870s and 1940s—the period on which the nomination papers focus— was marked by social, political, and economic segregation. Union was not unusual in this respect. As in many places across the United States, and especially in the South, churches, schools, social clubs, and cemeteries were segregated, jobs were divided along racial lines, and boundaries were demarcated between "whites" and "coloreds" in public spaces. This separation was in place in Union as well, and mirrored in residents' everyday social circles.

When black and white residents of Union came into contact with one another, it was usually in economically oriented transactions, often in the context of (white) employer and (black) employee. Nearly all the older African American women living in Union had worked as domestics in a white household at some point. Many of the men, too, had worked in the homes of white families as farm laborers, gardeners, or handymen. Even though black and white residents were interacting in the intimate spaces of private homes, and might share similar social and cultural values (see, e.g., Sobel 1987), the context of these interactions was highly stratified. As a result, neither black nor white residents tended to consider each other part of their own social realm. When current descendant residents recall the people who made up their social worlds, they do not mention the white residents who lived in Union. Similarly, delegitimized historians do not mention their black neighbors. A demographic mapping of Union at any time from 1870 might reveal a racially "mixed" settlement, but spatial mixing did not usually translate into social mixing in the past, and the same is arguably true today.

And so white residents found themselves on the sidelines of Union's formal history. What did this marginalization mean to these residents? Their response to the NRHP narrative, like the responses of Union's descendant residents and history brokers, was shaped by their relationship to history as a concept and to Union as a social space. In contrast with descendant residents, Union's delegitimized historians were not indifferent to honor by virtue of (a publicized mainstream) history. On the contrary, like Union's history brokers, many believed that historical knowledge is "important" and felt that their own ancestors were "historic" in that they were significant in shaping national historical processes. Returning to Pitt-Rivers's tripartite definition of honor, Union's delegitimized historians felt honor through their connection to history, and behaved in a way that they felt should command honor, but (in contrast with descendant residents) they were not paid honor by others—at least not to the extent that they had expected or hoped for.

To understand this sense of marginalization, it is worth exploring the delegitimized historians' relationship to history. Ernest Greene, a white former resident who was raised in Union, was born in 1913, and moved to Riverton in 1934, but maintains that Union is "home," and feels deeply rooted in the place and its history. Early in 2002 I called Mr. Greene to see if we could schedule an interview. Our conversation, which I expected would be a preliminary introduction, quickly turned into an oral history about Greene's family.

Though I asked relatively few questions, Mr. Greene volunteered an extensive and almost rehearsed biography of his family. With a kind of urgency that I did not witness among descendant residents, Mr. Greene provided me with genealogical lists of family members, including their full names and dates of birth and death. He told me that his cousin had written two books about his maternal and paternal genealogies that I might wish to consult, and was presently engaged in writing a third book that focuses on a collection of letters written by two "great-great-great-uncles," confederate soldiers during the Civil War. The following is an excerpt from my field notes:

[January 28, 2002] I called Ernest Greene, who was not only very enthusiastic to talk to me, but suggested that we do a series of conversations ("so I don't get too tired"), and was delighted that "a young person like myself" was interested in history. We talked for a good while, and I told him I was sorry I wasn't recording the conversation. "Once you turn the faucet on, it's hard to turn off," he joked. "But don't worry. I will repeat what I said today when you have the tape recorder."

Ernest Greene kept his promise and repeated everything he had shared with me over the phone—and more—during our meetings. I learned that he and his cousin Peter both engaged in researching and writing histories, and would regularly share insights about historical documents and materials they uncovered. Peter kept various artifacts from his mother's old house and things he picked up at garage sales and antique stores that were similar to items he remembered from his childhood. He organized these, along with a collection of old photographs inherited from his mother, into a sort of archive that he maintained in his basement. Ernest, for his part, was an avid reader and contributed his extensive knowledge of historical literature, especially about the Civil War.

It was obvious that the two cousins derived joy from learning about and recording history. Piecing together genealogies of their family is a hobby they indulged with vigor. In the time I spent with each of the cousins, the conversation rarely veered away from the subject of history, and when we did not meet for some time, Peter (and sometimes Ernest) would mail me copies of documents and photos that he had uncovered, along with notes describing any knowledge they had about the item—or asking if I could help identify a particular source.

In contrast with the descendant residents, the Greene cousins engaged regularly in the writing of history—in particular history that related directly to their own family. Neither cousin hesitated to share historical knowledge with me and, in fact, they gave me more materials than I knew what to do with. Akin to the descendant residents, Peter and Ernest Greene also thought that history was the recording of "important facts"—people, places, dates, and events—but contrary to descendant residents, they felt that their own family history qualified as history that was important and meaningful. The cousins did not necessarily think their family was unusually important, but stories about their lives and experiences were important enough to be recorded and disseminated.

The cousins' interest in the past—their collection of historical artifacts, their reading of history books, their genealogical recordings—might, on the surface, look similar to that of Union's history brokers. The two groups, history brokers and delegitimized historians, share the sense that learning about the past is "important." But while history brokers collect artifacts about a generalized past, using them as accessories to elevate their social status, delegitimized historians are entirely committed to the meticulous recording and archiving of particular artifacts, representing a specific past: their own. If delegitimized historians imagine their history as endowing them with a patina, it was of an entirely different quality than that of history brokers. For Ernest and Peter Greene, the act of collecting is steeped in a commitment to ensuring that the past is not forgotten, that records are created and kept and can be passed on to future generations, that those who came before will be remembered. For the most part, these residents share a common sense of historical dispossession: a sense that mainstream histories shed an unfavorable light on their ancestors and their past, and that these histories represent their ancestors as backward and racist.

From these residents' perspective, the single most important event in mainstream history—and the one most unfavorably represented by others—is the Civil War (or, as delegitimized historians sometimes prefer, the "War between the States"). Many delegitimized historians trace their own past to ancestors who fought for the Confederate army during the Civil War, or who supported the Confederacy. In contrast with the historical narratives often represented in mainstream venues (schools, the media, etc.), delegitimized historians read into the narratives about the Confederate army acts of patriotism, valor, and—most importantly—honor. Their own narratives about the war identify their ancestors as soldiers who were loyal to their army and state, war heroes who died defending their families and their land. Slavery is conveniently brushed aside in these narratives. As this version goes, the soldiers were poor and short on resources, yet they continued to fight against the odds, winning (there is special emphasis on this point) battle after battle—even if they did not ultimately win the war. Despite how mainstream histories frame this historical moment, the ultimate lesson that delegitimized historians take from the Civil War is about rugged autonomy, fierce independence, and fighting against the odds. As such, the valor, independence, and autonomy they read in the acts of their ancestral Confederate soldiers are seen by delegitimized historians as a metaphor for the values they themselves hold and wish to transmit to their progeny.

From the perspective of delegitimized historians, American society at large does not appreciate or even properly understand the honorable and patriotic acts of Confederate soldiers, and therefore they do not pay proper respect to those soldiers or their contemporary descendants. History, it is said, is written by the victors, and the Confederate army lost. Mainstream histories of the Civil War tend to focus on victory of the Union army, and especially on the abolition of slavery that resulted from it. In contrast, slavery and abolition are only rarely mentioned in the historical narratives by delegitimized historians, and if relations between blacks and whites are mentioned at all, the focus is frequently and surprisingly on the purportedly close relations between the two groups. More importantly, delegitimized historians are among those who believe that the South lost not only the physical battle, but the cultural one as well. These residents are acutely aware of the frequent depiction in media and popular discourse of Southerners as stupid, ignorant and, most damningly, racist.

In reaction, delegitimized historians developed an alternative discourse about heritage, history, and honor. Manifestations of this discourse can be found throughout the region, from the Confederate stars-and-bars flag (appropriately named the "rebel" flag) plastered proudly across vehicles' rear windows (sometimes accompanied by the expression "fear this"), to a multitude of Civil War reenactments around the area, to the persistent production of historical narratives that "correct" the unfavorable light in which the South is cast.

A sample of bumper stickers for sale at the Piedmont County fair articulates well this alternative discourse. Almost all sport a Confederate

Bumper stickers for sale at the Piedmont County fair. (Note especially "Restore Southern Heritage by educating the ignorant," "My heritage, your ignorance," and "I'd rather be historically accurate than politically correct.") Photo by Mieka Brand Polanco.

flag and include slogans such as "Restore Southern Heritage by educating the ignorant," "I'd rather be historically accurate than politically correct," and "These [flag's] colors don't run. Never have. Never will." Each of the slogans combines a reclamation (and renarration) of history, and an apparent disregard for what others (frequently reduced to "Yankees") might think. Together, these acts—displaying bumper stickers, reenacting battles, and especially (re)writing history—allow people like Union's delegitimized-historian residents to gain a sense of being paid honor, even if it is only among themselves.

Most of Union's delegitimized historians do not flaunt bumper stickers on their cars, but they do participate in challenging mainstream histories in other ways, as active members of the Sons of Confederate Veterans (SCV), by supporting local historical societies that affirm their own historical sensibilities, and by writing histories about their own ancestors.

"We owe it to the boys who were in the trenches," proclaimed the local SCV "camp commander" during a monthly meeting. "We owe it to them for everything that they went through and everything that they sacrificed."

Thus, these three groups—history brokers, descendant residents, and delegitimized-historian residents—will be explored in the following chapters, revealing the interplay of history, space, and race and whether they add up to community in one small town in Virginia.

Chapter Outline

The chapters that follow offer a study of the concept of "community" and how it is produced and experienced in one particular southern U.S. site, Union. As the above introduction to Union's residents suggests—and as this book will continue to argue—the ways in which communities are produced and experienced and the dynamics of history, space, and race differ for each of Union's resident groups. Each chapter explores how "community" is articulated by one of these groups—descendant residents, history brokers, and delegitimized historians—paying particular attention to how history, space, and race are primary components in the production of community.

Chapter 1, "Gating Union: The Politics of 'Protecting' Community," concentrates on history brokers in their production and experience of community. Focusing on an unveiling ceremony for the Union Historic District highway marker, the chapter examines the relationship that Union's history brokers have developed with Union as a Historic District—a relationship they presume is shared by other residents as well. It shows the unveiling ceremony for Union's historic highway as a ritualized process in which history brokers establish history as sacred. From this perspective, the "Union community" is conceived primarily as a physical landscape that encompasses history as well as race. With the baptism of Union as a Historic District, social and legal sanctions are enacted, fortifying it against potential land developers. But while history brokers act as the gatekeepers of history, descendant residents are endowed with the role of historic markers, authenticating with their presence Union's status as "historic."

Chapter 2, "Thick Histories: Producing Communities through Historical Narratives," focuses on "community" as it is produced and experienced by Union's descendant residents. This chapter considers some of the histories residents narrate in formal interview settings, alongside those that are shared during informal conversations. In informal settings residents narrate histories as fragments embedded in conversation about the present and repeated in different contexts. Each repetition inevitably varies slightly, highlighting particular aspects of a person or event depending on the context in which the story is told. Unlike the rigid narratives told during formal settings, this kind of historical transmission produces "thick" histories—three-dimensional and dynamic narratives that are continually produced, that are patently conscious of their relationship to the present, and that work to affirm a shared sense of community among the speakers.

Chapter 3, "'Not to Scale': Cartographic Productions of Community," focuses on expressions and productions of "community" among Union's delegitimized historians. Offering a detailed analysis of a map hand drawn by one such resident, this chapter considers how history, space, and race come together to form a sense of community that is unique to those identified as delegitimized historians. These residents are invested in the concept of official histories as a nationalist project, but they also tend to read themselves as invisible in these narratives. Ernest Greene, then 85 years old, drew a map of Union as he remembered it from his childhood. Unlike the NRHP history, which portrays Union as a relatively homogenous "black" space, Greene's map portrays an equally homogeneous "white" landscape. Not only were the homes, church, and school that constituted African American social terrain omitted, but the structures constituting white residents' domain were carefully stretched to abut each other, concealing any unaccounted-for blank spots on the map. I describe this cartographic act as a reflection of the delegitimized historians' productions and experiences of community—where an implicit recognition of historical documents as instruments of power is manifest. Historical documents are seen as both producing and legitimizing a relationship to place, which makes Greene's erasure of one portion of the population all the more poignant.

Finally, chapter 4, "Unfolding Community: Union Road as a 'Uniter of People'?," returns to a broad perspective of community as a concept in which history, space, and race are constantly "becoming" and where competing meanings are intertwined with and influenced by one another. Rather than thinking of the concept of community as fixed within each group, this chapter emphasizes community as a multilayered and complex experience. In Union residents operate within multiple and overlapping social circles, continually negotiating new productions and experiences of "community."

By offering insight into the ways history, space, and race operate within each of the social groups living in Union, this book builds a subtle reading into the politics of turning Union into a historically black community. It would be easy—but inaccurate—to say that history brokers are interested only in furthering their own goals regardless of the hopes and expectations of descendant residents; or that descendants are mere victims of an oppressive power structure whose own narratives are completely absent in the official history; or that the marginalization felt by delegitimized historians is nothing but a fiction of their own imaginations. Such statements, besides being incorrect, also ignore the delicate social fabric within which these three groups are nonetheless woven into each other's lives, forming sometimes surprisingly intimate social relationships within a single locale.

The chapters ahead bring into relief some of the complexities of the term "community" and how history, space, and race come to bear on this concept in a historically black U.S. community. There are few terms so central to the anthropological endeavor, and yet "community" is often glossed uncritically in the literature and without recognition of its myriad meanings. Despite its centrality, relatively few ethnographies focus on the concept of community (e.g., Redfield 1956; Tönnies 2001; Cohen 1985; Amit 2002). Rather than assuming that the term speaks for itself, and instead of imposing a single, fixed definition on it, this book explores the fluidity of community as it is composed and experienced by the ethnographic actors themselves. In focusing on Union, Virginia, this work highlights one particular range of possibilities as it unfolds in this particular site, while shining a light onto the sometimes obscure social, political, and economic structures that produce undeniably real experiences of class- and race-based disparities in the United States today.

2

Gating Union

The Politics of "Protecting" Community

Itself the outcome of past actions, social space is what permits
fresh actions to occur, while suggesting others and prohibit-
ing yet others.
Henri Lefebvre, *The Production of Space* (1991)

The Union Community Association is based on a sort of
"true" community. We worked really hard to develop a community identity. Because originally the idea of Union had
been dying out, so we worked very hard to resurrect it. Now
community maps show Union—and that didn't used to happen a few years ago. It's just popping up on maps everywhere.
Michael Taps, Union resident

There are no physical markers that delineate Union's boundaries. Brick
walls do not fortify it against its surrounding neighbors, nor do iron gates
control the movement of traffic at the edge of the two roads leading into
it. There are no physical boundaries around Union, and yet one could
argue that the social and legal codes that formed as a result of NRHP
identifying this place as a Historic District are in some ways just as real
as iron fences or brick walls. In this chapter I focus on the relationship
that Union's history brokers have with Union, and their work to produce

the place as one sort of community. Specifically, I examine how Union is produced and experienced as a place bound by its relationship to official history and to the state. This double bind allows some residents to enjoy the luxury of rustic living at the edge of urban development, while confining others to an economic wasteland in the midst of prosperity.

The labor invested by Union's history brokers into producing Union as an official "historically black community" has transformed the place into a gated community in every sense of the term. Much in the same way that "conventional" gated communities produce a (possibly false) sense of security among residents by fortifying the landscape against unwanted intruders (e.g., Blakely and Snyder 1997; Caldeira 2000; Low 2001, 2003; Horst and Brand 2008), Union's state-sanctioned historic status erects socioeconomic barriers that prevent unwanted intrusions and generally restrict movement into and out of the community without ever having to resort to physical gates or walls.

The process of gaining official recognition for Union as a Historic District has essentially "gated out" potentially marauding land developers. But while historic recognition might have ultimately benefited all residents to some degree, it was a process in which only history brokers were the legitimate authors of the official history. As I show in the next pages, in the process of producing the officially sanctioned NRHP historical narrative, descendant residents were present merely as historical artifacts, objects of the historical gaze, but not themselves partners in the official narration.

This chapter focuses on one particular event, the unveiling ceremony for the historic highway marker, as a ritualized moment in which legal and social barriers are erected against outside intruders. I outline this process with reference to symbolic anthropologist Victor Turner's works on rites of passage, showing that history is established in this context as sacred (that is, something that is "protected and isolated by prohibitions" [Durkheim 2008:40]), and history brokers therefore imagine the protection of a historic Union as their civic and moral duty. The ceremony, a rite of passage in which Union is transformed from an unmarked locale into a historically black community, is a process in which descendant residents become unintentional stand-in ritual subjects, human embodiments of the historical landscape.

There are three premises for this analysis that grow directly out of my experiences with Union's residents. The first is that Union's residents and the state each think of historic-ness in slightly different ways. How do we know whether a place is "historic"—and especially whether it is sufficiently historic for official state recognition? Using the NRHP definition of the term, sites are "historic" if they are "significant in American history, archeology, architecture, engineering, or culture." But significance, of course, is a deeply subjective term that is evaluated differently by the state than by the residents.

My second premise is that the desire to preserve the past is not universal. Preservation reifies the state as the guardian of tradition (Anderson 2006:186), and facilitates its ability to manage the terms under which the past becomes known (Trouillot 1995:113–18). Organizations like the NRHP often claim (and academia usually reiterates) that history is "important," but the questions "why?" and "to whom?" are often left unasked. Union's descendant residents, whose ancestors were the very justification for historic recognition, were far less enthusiastic about preserving Union's history than the history brokers who oversaw the recognition process. Descendant residents did not object to their past being remembered or officially recognized, but the nature of their relationship to history—why it matters, or even if it matters—was distinctly different from that of history brokers.

The final premise is that the relationship between history and space is in continual flux. Space cannot be frozen in time and neither can history—even if they are publicly imagined to possess this ability. Both history and space are continually being transformed in their own way. The landscape changes, buildings get older, some collapse, some are utilized in new ways, greenery (the bushes) conceals abandoned homes or is cut away to expose new contours in the terrain. And history changes, too. New events are recorded, older events lose significance or are elevated to mythic proportions, new narrators find different points to emphasize, or highlight connections between heretofore unrelated events. And yet the boundaries around Historic Districts are imagined as "protecting" history, keeping it from being contaminated by influences that are perceived as un-historic.[1]

The Unveiling Ceremony for Union as a Historic District

More than three years in the making, recognition for Union, Virginia, as a Historic District was officially conferred in 1999 by the National Register of Historic Places. Prior to granting this state-sanctioned recognition, the Union Community Association hired two professional historians who, over the course of a year, conducted research and wrote a comprehensive report on Union's social and architectural history. Many of Union's history brokers also contributed their own time and knowhow to collecting relevant materials, organizing scattered information, and tediously completing the nomination papers required for official recognition. In an early-spring ceremony in 2000, the new historic highway marker was unveiled—and also revealed were some of the latent ironies and tensions embedded within Union's new identity as a historically black community.

The nomination papers outline various architectural and archival justifications for listing Union as a Historic District, noting that some of the descendants of those early "freed black slaves" continue to live within the district today, thereby making the community especially "historical." The nomination papers portray a place where both black and white residents have lived as early as the mid-18th century . . . and yet they describe this place as a "historically *black* community" (emphasis added). Nor do the nomination papers point out that while Union was being given a monochromatic racial identity, the history-broker residents responsible for historic recognition were themselves predominantly white. It was with some surprise, then, that during one of my early trips to Union I met with a white resident who proudly told me he lived in a "historically black community"—and though I did not think much of it at the time, his words continued to resonate as I realized that none of the black residents in Union seemed to make the same claim.

At the unveiling ceremony, black residents identified as "descendants of the founding families" were ushered to a position near the newly minted highway marker commemorating Union's new status. They stood by the marker for several minutes, posing for a picture-taking session while the history brokers stepped out of the frame in order to ensure the "authenticity" of the image—a historically black community legitimated by its black residents. Some history brokers who brought their own cameras joined the media photographers in recording the event, while others stood around casually chatting or enjoying the refreshments.

The scene at the ceremony—black residents posing around the historic marker while white residents recorded the event (making sure that whiteness did not inauthenticate the historical frame)—provides a powerful metaphor for some of the dynamics in the making of Union as a Historic District. Although as many as 75 percent of the current population of Union identify as "white," the site was recognized as representative of "black heritage." Moreover, while history brokers were busy with the tedious process of obtaining official historic recognition, descendant residents were asked to contribute mostly as storytellers or, strangely enough, simply by their presence as black residents.

History brokers felt it was important to record and publicly recognize Union's past. They took upon themselves the job of excavating Union's history, while descendant residents became part of the collection of artifacts that was uncovered. As artifacts, these residents (and their memories) provided the contents of the historic investigation: they were interviewed and videotaped, and their words and images enhanced an already impressive archive of letters, court records, and architectural analyses of the area. As artifacts, moreover, descendant residents became tangible symbols of the past. Gathering around the historic marker, an unobservant bystander may be forgiven for not noticing the subtle transformation in which descendant residents became mimetically endowed with the

Descendant residents posing by the Union historic marker. Photo by Christine Madrid French, 1999.

qualities of the sign they stood beside, themselves turning into historic markers.

Union's history brokers worked hard to ensure that the official historical narrative was respectful and fair to their neighbors, that the ugly imprints of racism were not concealed, and that the descendants approved of the final narrative and corroborated its details. But at no point did history brokers consider having the descendants as collaborators in the production of materials for the nomination process. For this they hired outside historians. To qualify as a Historic District, the nomination papers for the NRHP had to prove that Union featured the appropriate "historic" characteristics (outlined in the NRHP application instructions), and the narrative had to be compelling and distinct enough to convincingly make a case for Union's historic-ness.

Because Union's very recognition as a Historic District was at stake, there was no room for polite gestures. Descendent residents never really expressed a desire for public recognition of Union's "historic-ness" (in fact, as discussed below, most descendants were not entirely convinced that Union was "historic" at all), and besides, they lacked the training and experience to navigate the bureaucratic maze of the recognition process. Professional historians were hired to write the official history, and most of their work was done in the county courthouse and archives, not in face-to-face interactions with residents themselves. In an interview, one of the authors of the nomination papers explained this was a conscious choice because "oral histories can lead you astray." "To tell you the truth," she admitted, "the way I approach these projects [of NRHP nominations] is: first I go through the written documents. I pore through those and try to get as much information from those as possible. Then if I have specific questions I usually call the person up and ask them over the phone." In the case of Union, her go-to contacts for questions were Jordan Lawson and Michael Taps, two of Union's history-broker residents.

The historians, in consultation with the history brokers, completed the nomination papers in the appropriate language of historical legitimation[2] and in accordance with the discourse of the state—in this case, represented by the National Register of Historic Places—and in 1999 Union was finally granted the prized Historic District status.

When Union first received historic recognition, many of the descendant residents were flattered by the attention, but insisted that their history was not much different from that of other communities in the area. When I asked residents about this, they would usually name three or four nearby communities that claimed similar beginnings. Descendants would often tell me that their memories were "not especially important" or "not historic"—and the frequency with which I heard such comments resonated with my sense that different residents offered competing visions of what they considered to be "historic," and disparate motivations for wanting (or not wanting) Union to be officially recognized.

Union provides a telling lesson in the politics embedded in formal historic recognition, and in the process of gating communities through social and legal codes without a need for iron gates or brick walls. Why did history brokers feel it was important for Union to have a publicly sanctioned history? What was the relationship of Union's various residents to the very idea of history? And what have been the social, political, and economic ramifications of formal historic recognition?

The Unveiling Ceremony as a Rite of Passage

Symbolic analysis of the unveiling ceremony—a ritualized event—can help to begin answering these questions. Rituals are, as Turner once suggested, "decisive keys to the understanding of how people think and feel about relationships, and about the natural and social environments in which they operate" (1995:6). Analysis of the ceremony as a ritualized event is especially revealing when it takes into account that the participants represent disparate groups who do not always share cultural understandings. As we unlock expressions of social, political, and economic relationships held by Union residents, we also gain insight into some of the unspoken power dynamics embedded within the process of producing Union as a Historic District.

The unveiling ceremony for the historic highway marker was choreographed by Union's history brokers through the Community Association to mark Union's transition from an unmarked, semi-rural community at the edge of development into a formally recognized Historic District. Rites de passage, Turner writes, are said to "indicate and constitute transitions between states" (1970:93). In other words, the "ritual subjects" (to use his term) are understood to be in one culturally recognized state before they participate in the ritual, and in a new, different (and frequently higher [Turner 1975:232]) state when they are reincorporated into society. And while Turner's ritual subjects are identified as individuals or groups, I show here that place, too, can be a ritual subject undergoing transition from one culturally recognized state to another. At the culmination of the rite of passage, Union, the ritual subject, fills a new social personhood, a new state, and "by virtue of this, has rights and obligations vis-à-vis others of clearly defined 'structural' types; he is expected to behave in accordance with certain customary norms and ethical standards binding on incumbents of social position in a system of such positions" (Turner 1995:95).

Changing States: From Undifferentiated Suburb to Historic District

Before Union was officially recognized as a Historic District, it was mostly indistinguishable from its surrounding landscape. Located in predominantly rural Piedmont County, Union is not unlike many small settlements in central Virginia: a small cluster of new and old houses loosely organized along a winding country road. Passersby usually notice Mt. Zion Baptist Church sitting on a small hill beside Union Road, but even residents are hard pressed to define where Union ends and another place begins.

In their everyday life, Union's exact boundaries are unimportant to residents—especially those who grew up in Union or whose families had been living in the area for some generations. To these people Union is "home," an ever-evolving site of sociality, a place of memories, of intimacy, of what French philosopher Gaston Bachelard describes as the "profound reality of all the subtle shadings of our attachment to a chosen spot" (1994:4). Before urban development began dissolving the outer edges of this place, Union had been a distinctly rural and relatively self-sufficient settlement with two or three general stores, a post office, and a railroad station, and one where residents raised and grew much of their own food. On occasion some residents would go on a special outing to the nearby city of Riverton, taking a now-defunct train line to go shopping or see a movie, but would otherwise spend most of their time in and around Union.

With the growth of a reliable road system, Union began attracting newcomers, since it could offer out-of-the-way serenity, but also relative proximity to slightly more urban centers. Residents could now rely on private transportation for easy access to commerce and employment opportunities. But as it became more attractive as a residential space, Union's social and commercial spaces began disappearing so that today there are no stores in Union, no commerce, and no social centers outside the church. As a community that is essentially exclusively residential, Union today is mostly indistinguishable from the growing suburban settlements by which it is surrounded.

In its post-recognition state, the Union Historic District holds a new set of social "rights and obligations" that it did not have before. An excerpt from the NRHP website helps illustrate this point. The site states:

- Listing in the National Register *honors the property* by recognizing its importance to its community, state, or the Nation.
- Federal agencies, whose projects affect a listed property, must give the Advisory Council on Historic Preservation an opportunity to comment on the project and its effects on the property. [. . .]
- Owners of listed properties *may be able to obtain Federal historic preservation funding*, when funds are available. In addition, Federal investment tax credits for rehabilitation and other provisions may apply.
- Owners of private property listed in the National Register have no obligation to open their properties to the public, to restore them, or even to maintain them, if they choose not to do so. Owners can do anything they wish with their property provided that no Federal license, permit, or funding is involved. (NRHP 1993, emphasis added)

Even though some nearby settlements share a past similar to Union's, the fact that Union underwent a rite of passage and was recognized as a Historic District means that it embodies the state of being "historic," and therefore is constrained (or liberated) by specific rights and obligations. Union continues to be "home," a site of sociality, memories, and intimacy, but now the old houses are also officially recognized as "contributing structures" to the historic listing, Union now appears on local maps and is even referred to by county government as a "model community" in their plans for future development. The Virginia Tourism Corporation also now includes Union as a destination on their African American Heritage Trail.

Union as Bounded Space

Most importantly, Union as a Historic District now has clearly defined and absolute boundaries. "All margins are dangerous," writes anthropologist Mary Douglas. "If they are pulled this way or that, the shape of fundamental experience is altered. Any structure of ideas is vulnerable at its margins" (1984:122). If Union's margins were vulnerable or in danger of allowing the "shape of fundamental experience" to be altered (for example, by allowing suburban development to take over a lone bastion of rural living), its historic status ensured that this would not happen.

The NRHP's nomination papers detail precisely where Union's boundaries lie and are accompanied by accounts of each structure within it. Some structures are now distinctly within the margins of the Historic District, while others are indisputably outside it. Likewise, some people live inside the Union Historic District, while others do not. Ironically, because the NRHP insists that Historic Districts consist of a certain ratio of "contributing" versus "noncontributing" structures—and because so many new houses were erected there in the late 19th century—the official boundaries around the Union Historic District are a bizarre set of zigzags that does not correspond to what any resident would actually consider the Union community. The official boundaries were drawn to adhere to the required concentration of "contributing structures" and subsequently exclude some older houses belonging to residents who would certainly have been considered part of the community in previous times. Nonetheless, Union's margins have been identified and secured. Boundaries now exist around the Historic District, and it is precisely these boundaries that keep land developers from building new, high-density subdivisions in Union, as explained further below.

Union (as ritual subject) undergoes the full ritual process in order to fill its new, elevated state as a Historic District. "Rites characteristically begin with the subjects being symbolically killed or separated from ordinary secular or profane relationships, and conclude with a symbolic birth or reincorporation into society," writes Turner (1975:53). "The intervening liminal period or phase is thus betwixt and between the categories of ordinary life." But because not all participants in the ritual share the same cultural values—namely, the same investment in formal history— the liminal phase is also when power disparities begin appearing on the social landscape.

Liminality: Taking Space out of Time

According to Turner, the middle phase of the rite of passage, liminality, is "a 'moment in and out of time,' and in and out of secular social structure" (1995:96). As suggested above, with the commencement of the unveiling ceremony, Union is no longer simply an unmarked locality slowly dissolving into suburban development (its preliminal state)—but it is also not quite yet a full-fledged Historic District (its postliminal state). Union is on its way to transitioning into its new state as a Historic District. It is at this stage also that the participants in the ceremony become stand-ins for the locality, themselves experiencing the "betwixt and between" of liminality.

To mark the symbolic separation of the sacred from the profane, Union's history brokers chose Mt. Zion Baptist Church—the church that had been hand built in 1891 by members of Union's "founding families," and where most of Union's descendant residents had worshipped over the years—as the site for the unveiling ceremony. Besides being a ritual space designated for spiritual learning and fellowship, the church is also a place where worshippers are "born again" (through baptism) into Christianity, and where last rites are held at death. Birth, life, and death—a complete life cycle—is represented in the church, an appropriate space for liminality, which is "frequently likened to death, to being in the womb" (Turner 1995:95).

Congregating in the sanctuary, and opening with a prayer led by Mt. Zion's pastor, the ceremony participants—history brokers, descendant residents, and even the small audience of journalists and well-wishers— are all transported into ritual space and time. Indeed, participants are transported into a ritual space out of time: "The historic highway marker sign that has brought us here today is a physical and public reminder of the unique history of this place and the people who have called it home," remarks the Union Community Association's president. The church becomes a space where the past is indistinguishable from the present, "the place" and "the people" are one, and the historical narrative, the highway marker, and the descendants all become metonyms for one another. It is also a space in which structural distinctions of age, race, class, and (noteworthy given the location) religious convictions are temporarily set aside, making room for what Turner calls communitas, a "modality of social relationship" that is unstructured, undifferentiated and based on an "essential and generic human bond" (Turner 1995:95–96).

But if, as argued earlier, Union (the place), is the ritual subject, why is it that the participants at the ceremony (the people) are those who experience communitas? This discrepancy is reflective of the social nature of space, of space that is both the site for social production, but also a product of it. Social space is "at once a precondition and a result of social superstructures" (Lefebvre 1991:85). In other words, although Union is the ritual subject, as a "place" it is much more than simply a geographical location. Place, writes social geographer Yi-Fu Tuan, is space that is endowed with (cultural) value (2002). Place "implies, contains and dissimulates" social relations (Lefebvre 1991:83): at the unveiling ceremony, the social relations implied, contained, and dissimulated in the ritual are inextricably linked to the space within which they occur.

Union, the ritual subject that transitions into the new "Historic District" state, is also necessarily its social meaning—the social relationships that made Union into a place in the past, and the values that give it meaning as a historic place in the present. It could be argued that Union embodies that illusive idea that some call "community." It is precisely because social space is an accumulation of social relationships embedded within the physical landscape that the participants in the ceremony can act as stand-in ritual subjects for Union. And more, because the relationships that make up Union are ongoing, continually informing and being informed by the space within which they occur, stand-in ritual subjects are not limited only to "descendant residents" or even only to residents at all. Instead, all participants in the ritual—outside observers as well as the residents themselves—come to stand in for Union, the authentic ritual subject.

Protecting Sacred Space

The logistics of wrestling physical space into ritual subject-hood can become quite complicated when the time comes to perform an actual, lived (and experienced) ritual. Instead, when history brokers planned the unveiling ceremony, they had to find a tangible symbol that would represent all that they felt Union had been in the past—and that could contain all that came with its new historic status in the future. Union's history brokers did not have to look far to find what they considered to be the perfect symbol for their purposes: their black neighbors. In this act, which history brokers surely imagined as honoring the descendant residents, we gain the first glimpse of a rite of passage gone awry.

From the moment the pastor begins reciting his opening prayer until one of the descendant residents makes the final benediction, the participants—all participants—exist in ritual liminality. The sacred/profane dichotomy is elementary both during this phase, and in what will soon be Union's new state as a Historic District. And rites of passage are society's way of articulating the distinction between what it considers to be sacred and what, on the other hand, is considered profane.

The ceremony allows the ritual practitioners to establish unambiguously that history is sacred, and can now be "protected and isolated by prohibitions" from its profane surroundings (Durkheim 2008:40). Union may abut urban development, planned communities, new construction, and other perceived antitheses of history, but its margins have been buttressed and secured, ensuring that any potential marauders are rendered impotent within Union through carefully defined socio-legal boundaries.

At the unveiling ceremony, history is established as sacred, and history is metonymized by the presence of black descendant residents.

To reiterate the distinction made in the preface, it is not the past—social processes that took place in prior moments—that is held sacred. Rather, it is history—the narrative about the past—around which the ceremony revolves. In the poignant anecdote quoted earlier, Michael Taps, Union Community Association president, notes that the unveiled highway marker is a "public reminder of the unique history of this place and the people who have called it home." It is not necessary for him to point out that the people who call it home refers specifically to African American residents. Quite subtly, by noting Union's "unique history," the speaker already implies their racial identity (for what makes Union "unique" according to the nomination papers is its contribution to history in the area of "Ethnic Heritage—Black"). Taps continues, "[The highway marker] represents the success of the Union community in its efforts to document its history and gain recognition of Union and its story" (emphasis added). Not the past, but the documentation of it is signified by the highway marker. Not the past, but "its story."

Historic Markers

There is nothing particularly novel or intrinsically problematic about holding a historical narrative to be sacred. Indeed, there are many religions whose central sacred text is a historical narrative.[3] What is important in this analysis, however, is that Union's history brokers establish during the unveiling ceremony a sacred reverence not simply for a historical narrative, but for the very idea of history. This is evident not only in the content of the speech delivered by Michael Taps (himself one of Union's history brokers), but in the very nomination papers for the National Register of Historic Places.

According to the nomination papers, Union's claim to significance is that it is "the best preserved and the most thoroughly documented historically black community in the region." The wording does not indicate that Union is noted for being unusual or outstanding in some way, but merely that it has existed for a long time and that written records can corroborate this fact ("best preserved" and "most thoroughly documented"). Although Union was ultimately recognized as a Historic District, it is described in the nomination papers as "historical" and not "historic." In other words, it is a place that contains evidence of the past (historical), but not necessarily a place of lasting significance (historic).[4] Even though the place does not exhibit especially unique or outstanding characteristics (at least according to the NRHP nomination papers), the very fact that its past is documented is enough to warrant official historic standing.

Equally important, what was understood as "historical" was extended beyond mere documentation of past moments to include also current, living residents of Union. Since Union was identified as a Historic District within the area of significance "Ethnic Heritage—Black," Union's history brokers apparently felt it would be appropriate to have "ethnically black" people representing the new title. As long as the ceremony stayed within the church building, everyone in the room could be considered a participant in the ritual throughout the speeches and remarks. However, once the group poured out onto the lawn for the actual unveiling of the highway marker and a picture-taking session, only those who were identified as descendants continue to perform the role of stand-in ritual subjects. This is the final phase of the rite of passage, post-liminality, and descendant residents are the only ones to undergo "symbolic birth or reincorporation into society" (Turner 1975:53).

In a barely noticeable shift, white history brokers bow out of the ritual process, leaving the black descendants alone to be "reborn and reincorporated" as historical subjects. Absurd as it may seem, the residents who were identified as descendants, standing in for Union as it underwent the ritual process, themselves became permanent markers of history once the ritual was over. Turner notes that a ritual subject's final, post-liminal state—like the liminal phase itself—also contains sacred characteristics (1995:97). African American residents who had been identified as "descendants" were no longer merely residents of Union (as white residents could continue to be), they were now symbols of Union's sacred historic-ness.

This point calls into question the issue of precisely whose social values and beliefs were guiding the unveiling ceremony. It should not be surprising to learn that Union's black residents—descendants or otherwise—did not tend to think of themselves as historical markers. Descendants were pleased to have their ancestors recognized in the ceremony and on the highway marker, but most did not read into the event the same meanings that history brokers did. Even Joanne Mitchel, the speaker identified as "spokesperson for descendants"—and one of the few descendant residents who is also a Community Association member—neglected to honor history (as a concept) in her remarks. In her comments she points out that her great-great-grandfather was "one of the original African Americans who helped settle and develop the Union community," and says she is "proud, honored, and blessed" to be celebrating the event with her family. She does not suggest that history itself should be an object of honor. In fact, when she uses the term "historic" in her speech, it is to describe the present ("this historic event") and to imply grandeur, not past-ness.

Establishing the "Right Relationship" to History

We can now return to a point made earlier and begin to unlock its meaning, namely, that while Union's white history-broker residents expressed pride in the fact that they lived in a "historically black community," black descendant residents never made the same claim. These residents certainly engaged in producing their own set of narratives about the past (as described in chapter 3), but if Union's status as a formally recognized Historic District was mentioned at all (and it rarely was), it was usually followed by a semi-interested shrug. Clearly, "history" was especially sacred to Union's history brokers, while descendant residents held a different relationship to the past and to narratives about it. The process of gaining official recognition from the NRHP was one in which descendant residents served only as historical artifacts, narrated about but not themselves partners in the narration of the history told about them. Descendant residents produced—and continue to produce—narratives about their past (as discussed in the next chapter), but these were not offered to the NRHP as representative histories. Instead, the official history of Union submitted to the NRHP was written by "professional" historians in the hegemonic language that would be most likely to gain Union official historic recognition.

But it was not only this act of exclusion that promoted descendants' disinterest in Union's historic status once the ceremony was over. Union's white history brokers considered official history a site of legitimation, a kind of collective, national creation-myth that revered "important" people and events that they considered part of their own past. These residents drew a sense of pride and national belonging from historical narratives. By grafting a history of Union's African American residents onto the national history narrative, Union's history brokers imagined themselves doing the right thing, by giving honor where honor has long been overdue. It is no small feat to gain historic recognition by the NRHP, and the effort that history brokers invested into obtaining this status for Union was one way they could clarify to their black neighbors that they appreciated and respected their history.

Union's descendant residents, on the other hand, did not tie their sense of identity and self-worth to an official or national history—they drew their sense of identity from sources such as their families, and self-worth was closely linked to their ability to labor. The honor that history brokers bestowed upon them by making them into historic markers was therefore not necessarily appreciated by descendant residents. Descendant residents were not offended by the gesture (though they could have read it as patronizing), but neither did they experience the same sacred reverence towards history that the history brokers felt. Simply stated, most descendant residents did not care much about how history was narrated, or by whom.

A successful rite of passage, according to Turner, "establish[es] a right relationship between involuntary sentiments and the requirements of social structure. People are induced to want to do what they must do" (1974:56). In the case of Union, transition into the state of Historic District-hood was completed, but the stand-in ritual subjects were not "successfully" induced into the proper relationship with official history. Descendants did not consider themselves historical markers, nor did they appear to revere history in the same way that history brokers did. Fortunately for history brokers, in order to gain formal historical recognition, descendant residents did not need to do much other than continue to live in Union, legitimating its historic identity by their presence.

The Historic Listing in Social and Political Perspective

Why were history brokers so intent on producing and then protecting Union's history? What was so profane about Union's surroundings that they felt compelled to separate themselves from the outside with these historical barriers? To answer this, an understanding is needed of the political and economic context within which Union was officially recognized as a Historic District. Like all counties in Virginia, Piedmont County is required to produce a comprehensive plan that outlines "the physical development of the territory within its jurisdiction." The Code of Virginia states, "The comprehensive plan shall be made with the purpose of guiding and accomplishing a coordinated, adjusted and harmonious development of the territory which will, in accordance with present and probable future needs and resources, best promote the health, safety, morals, order, convenience, prosperity and general welfare of the inhabitants" (§15.2-2223).

Every six years, county planning commissioners review and adjust any such "present and probable future needs" in light of new conditions that have emerged. The review process, which even during uneventful years tends to expose fissions among the politically appointed commissioners, was especially rancorous in 1996 with a new proposal to allocate large tracts of the county to development. Although the vast majority of the county had been—and continues to be—rural (that is, lightly populated, relatively undeveloped, and most importantly, zoned "rural" by the county government), as a whole Piedmont County had been experiencing a spurt of population growth that was making commissioners wary. Planning commissioners feared that without curbing developers' actions, Piedmont County would quickly become a landscape of sprawling suburbs. To prevent this, a growth management plan was devised to assign limited areas in the county for development, while "protecting the elements that define the Rural Area" in the rest of the land. In practical terms, this meant that development areas would be promoted as "the place where a variety of land uses, facilities, and services exist and are planned" (Piedmont County Comp Plan 1996:17). The idea was that commercial and economic resources would be concentrated in designated areas while the rest of the county would maintain its rural character.

When wealthy landowners around the county caught wind of the plan, they were outraged. They felt that the growth management plan was a trick designed by the county government, whose real agenda was to encourage massive population growth and suburban sprawl. Commissioners argued to the contrary. Designating specific development areas, they argued, was a way to curb growth by confining it to a limited area. Wealthy landowners (many of whom lived in expansive estates boasting vineyards and horse farms) were not convinced, especially when they saw "multi-family units" cropping up around them at a density of up to ten dwellings per acre. They were especially angered by plans for new business and commercial structures, civic centers, parking lots, public transit infrastructure, and other public spaces in the areas that had been designated for "growth."

An organization was formed for the express purpose of preventing development in Piedmont County (demanding a "sustainable population" was their preferred motto), and some of Union's history brokers became members. Comparing Piedmont's growth rate to that of China, India, and "the Whole World," the organization's glossy brochure warns fellow residents that growth must be harnessed "before it further erodes our quality of life" (OSP). Planning Commission board meetings, which at other times are almost painfully dull, became an arena for high emotion, heated arguments, and overall frustration, especially during the public hearing portion of the meetings. Commissioners who sided with anti-development sentiments claimed to speak on behalf of "the people," while commissioners who favored the development areas said they represented "working-class residents." In reality, the interests they represented were neither those of the "people," of the "working class," nor of an average Piedmont County resident. "I am probably going to vote against all growth areas," stated one anti-development commissioner. "I have been to every public meeting we have held and listened to hundreds of citizens, and with very few exceptions—in the business community and developers—I find absolutely no support [for development areas]. . . . I am not willing, at this point, to go ahead and vote against all those people" (Piedmont County PC 12/19:231). A pro-development commissioner articulated the opposite position by arguing that growth would mean more affordable housing:

> We can't stop people from coming here and we can't stop babies from being born. . . . [Voting against the development areas] is a travesty to the people who want to live here but have a hard time affording houses within this community. . . . I can't support this. I think this is unfair to the average working man in this community to do this. (Piedmont County PC 12/19:229)

To be sure, neither side was representing who they purported to represent. "The people" whom anti-development commissioners represented were wealthy landowners who felt that development areas threatened their property values and quality of life. Pro-development commissioners were supporting powerful land developers for whom every increase in density allowance meant they could build and sell more houses (houses that were, incidentally, beyond the reach of most county residents). Notably, despite the politicians' diplomatic wording, neither side made any gestures towards protecting or even considering the best interest of those who were neither rich nor powerful.

Union residents found themselves at the heart of the controversy, for coincidentally Union was designated for inclusion in one of those contentious development areas. Abutting what was already one of the largest subdivisions in Piedmont County,[5] Union was destined to be subsumed into one of the new development areas proposed by the county government. The outrage against growth expressed by wealthy homeowners in the county was shared by some of Union's residents as well.

Just at this time—in the heat of negotiations over Piedmont County's decision about the development areas—plans to gain official historic recognition for Union began to form. Initially, a group of Union residents requested that the Planning Commission redraw development area boundaries to exclude Union. Residents prepared speeches that cited every concern from "traffic, overcrowded schools, insufficient water supply, waste disposal and lack of employment opportunities" to fear for the preservation of natural areas. Some residents suggested that other parts of the county would be more amenable to development. But by far the most remarkable appeal came from a resident who identified himself as a member of the Union Community Association. In a prepared statement, this resident drew on language from the Piedmont Comprehensive Plan, reminding commissioners that one of the county's goals is to protect "historic and cultural resources" in the rural areas (Piedmont County Comp Plan 1996:3). "To Union residents," this speaker appealed,

> [growth] would mean that our community, now more than 120 years old, will lose its identity and its sense of place entirely. Existing land-use patterns which have not changed fundamentally since the Civil War would begin to more closely parallel those of the adjacent subdivision. The rural landscape, with important surviving remnants of a 19th century village would disappear in the wake of increased housing, business and traffic. . . . A recently completed Virginia Division of Historic Resources survey has identified the Village of [Union] as one of six eligible for listing on the National Register of Historic Places and the Virginia Landmarks Register. (Piedmont County PC 11/21:5)

These remarks, made almost three years prior to the unveiling ceremony, reveal some residents' first inklings of the need to protect Union's history. The idea of history as barricade was not quite formed, but these remarks provide insight into an early concern among some regarding potential marauders threatening the community.

Luckily—or not—for Union residents, appeals about Union's historical significance apparently resonated with the county commissioners. Less than a month after the residents' appeal at the public hearing, Union was dropped from the development area boundaries. Commissioners noted that it was "deleted as being less amenable [than other areas]." Even though they had achieved their goal, some residents were apparently shaken enough by the ordeal that they felt the need to erect a more formal and permanent barrier around Union: they would protect Union's history—and that history, in turn, would protect residents' properties and lifestyles. The newly formed Union Community Association established regular meetings in which participants discussed the community's future—and past—and plans were launched to apply to the National Register of Historic Places for official recognition as a Historic District. The professional historian hired to write the NRHP nomination papers explained this decision: "Well, the major incentive was to fend away developers. That was the main reason people were really pushing to do it [the Historic District nomination]."

Years later, in 2002, sitting in a quiet café in downtown Riverton, Jordan Lawson, then president of the Union Community Association, underscored this point to me. Union had already received its historical status at this point, but I knew that Mr. Lawson considered NRHP recognition to be part of a broader sustained effort to preserve Union's character. "We're not living at the end of the mountain track," he explained. "We're at the hard edge of the development area—but we are rural. And this is really where all the action is going to be in terms of discussion and thought and [action] at the county level." Later that day, Mr. Lawson would urge UCA members to harness their collective energy and prevent the nearby subdivision from encroaching upon the Union Historic District.

Gating Union

Returning to the earlier discussion of ceremony as a rite of passage, we recall that the ritual practitioners—Union's history brokers—treated history with sacred reverence. In negotiating with planning commissioners, we learn that they, too, held history to be a value that evoked reverence. To wit, a traveler through Piedmont County (and many nearby counties) will find a landscape dotted with small and large shrines to history. Silver highway markers—like the one now adorning the Mt. Zion Church lawn—bejewel roadsides and building fronts. Statues commemorating famous and less-famous Civil War soldiers guard crossroads and parks around the county. A televised commercial warns viewers against favoring usable space over historic sites. "No one looks back fondly on the time they spent in a parking garage," warns a voiceover as faux-1950s-fuzzy images of a happy (and multiracial!) group of schoolchildren fade into an image of a concrete, multitiered parking lot. "When you lose a historic place, you lose a part of who you are." And overshadowing all of these is the nearby crème de la crème of historic shrines, Thomas Jefferson's Monticello—not only a Historic District, but a World Heritage Site.

Life in Union did not change significantly as a result of its official recognition as a Historic District. Union did not suddenly become a hub of tourist interest or scholarly attention. In fact, it is quite possible that I was the only one to become interested in Union as a result of the recognition. The landscape changed only in that a historic marker now stands on the lawn of Mt. Zion Church, traffic speed within the district's boundaries was reduced from 40 to 30 miles per hour, and a general recommendation was issued to residents to avoid tampering with or destroying historical structures (an actual restriction could not legally be placed as the structures sit on privately owned land). But it is precisely the unchanging nature of the landscape that was so precious to history brokers that it warranted containing it within "sacred" margins.

"The sacred thing is, par excellence, that which the profane must not and cannot touch with impunity," writes French sociologist Émile

"Take a Ride Through History." History as recreational activity. Virginia's Retreat in Blue Ridge Outdoors, 2002.

Durkheim (2008:39). If history is indeed sacred, as I have argued it is to Union's history brokers, then what is the profane that "must not and cannot" touch it? In Union's case, it is development. The lines carefully drawn on area maps delineating the Union Historic District may not have a physical counterpart on the land, but they have very real manifestation in the social, political, and economic landscape. After some deliberation, planning commissioners decided to add the deceptively innocuous provision to the comprehensive plan stating that "a major upgrade of [Union Road] . . . is not recommended" (Piedmont County Comp Plan 1996:91). The goals of the history brokers were achieved.

When confronted with potential marauders, Union's history brokers chose to define and then fortify their community by erecting historical barriers. Blackness—which was offered by residents who were identified as "descendants"—became the tangible representation, and therefore the legitimation, for Union's history. History brokers, for their part, took on the role of gatekeepers, ensuring that history buffered the community against potential developers, and ensuring that their rustic lifestyle was safely guarded against the threat of development.

But while this arrangement worked well for history brokers who were relatively wealthy and had access to private transportation, it was less than perfect for everyone else. Historic recognition ensured that land developers were securely gated out, but so was any potential for commercial enterprise. Thus, historical recognition sealed Union's fate as a strictly residential suburb. While black residents were gated into Union as historical artifacts, potential employers and easy access to commerce and sociality were gated out. This was only too evident by the fact that all work-aged descendent residents moved away—most directly into the neighboring development area.

While younger residents were systematically moving away from Union, older residents—including those whose presence is supposed to legitimate Union's historic status—have found access to a social world beyond their home increasingly difficult. Jim Gaines, for example, had given up driving his car because of his age (87 when the unveiling ceremony was held) and failing eyesight—but for some time he continued to drive his small ride-lawnmower around Union and to a nearby convenience store. With grocery stores zoned out of the Historic District, Mr. Gaines found himself completely dependent on neighbors for his most basic shopping needs. He would now have to travel some five miles, including a multilane highway, to get to the nearest grocery store, a trip impossible given his mode of transportation. Those who frequented Mr. Gaines's house knew to call ahead and ask whether he needed any groceries.

His support system may have ensured a fairly secure source of groceries, but Mr. Gaines's opportunities to interact socially were dramatically curtailed as a result of Union's socio-legal barriers. Even the bus chartered to take aging residents to a nearby senior center stopped passing through Union, allegedly because it was out of the way and not worth the detour. Busses picked up senior citizens from the nearby development area, but one senior resident in Union found himself dependent on his circle of friends and family to maintain a social life beyond his home.

"Listing properties in the National Register often changes the way communities perceive their historic places," reads the NRHP brochure online. "Listing honors a property by recognizing its importance to its community, state, or the Nation" (NRHP 2004). Listing Union as a Historic District has certainly changed the way Union residents "perceive their historic place." It has even changed the ways county government, developers, and non–Union residents perceive it as well. Union is now a place that the state has deemed significant—though in a somewhat tenuous and abstract way. But it is also a place in which change has been artificially hindered; where some residents can think of themselves as guardians of history; where other residents might wonder where their voices fit into the official historical narrative; where land developers know they may not set their aspirations; and where I, a researcher, can now go (and with assurance, for the Union Historic District has absolute boundaries confirming that I am, indeed, in Union) and ask residents to share with me their history of the community.

In many ways Union's past is not especially unique or historic, but it is precisely this aspect that provides an insightful lesson in the study and politics of history and space in the United States. Descendant residents were appreciative of the interest in their past, but did not experience the same pride over historical recognition that was experienced by history brokers. Leaving them out as narrators in the official history compounded the schism, reinforcing white residents' role as authors of official history and black residents as artifacts. And while historic recognition was intended to honor black residents, the more immediate outcome was the gating out of an evolving social landscape.

Union is a place where the voices that celebrate African American history drown out the voices of present-day African American residents. While the recent trend to acknowledge African American history as a legitimate part of American history is certainly welcome and long overdue, it is only meaningful to those who feel invested in the narrative, either through reverence towards history as an idea, or simply by being included as partners in the narration.

Given their absence as narrators in the official history of Union, then, what are the histories that are narrated by Union's descendant residents? The following chapter explores historical narratives that are shared among these residents, narratives which, I will argue, are significantly different from those told by history brokers. The difference is manifested in the nature of the narratives, the context in which they are told, and the ways narratives about the past work to produce sociality. The qualitative difference between histories told by history brokers and those told by descendant residents is indicative not only of a different kind of relationship each resident group has to history and the past, but of a difference in the very way descendant residents and history brokers produce and experience community.

3

Thick Histories

Producing Community through Historical Narratives

Every corner of space conceals a multitude of individuals each
of whom totalizes the trend of history in a manner which
cannot be compared to others. . . . Even history which claims
to be universal is still only a juxtaposition of a few local histories in which (and between which) very much more is left
out than is put in.
Claude Lévi-Strauss, *The Savage Mind* (1966)

JIM GAINES: You got a picture of [the 1920s mail carrier] in
the buggy?
MIEKA: Yeah!
JIM GAINES: That's good. Now that's real history.
Interview with Jim Gaines, Union resident

In 1935, in one of the first ethnographies written about an African American community, anthropologist Zora Neale Hurston reflected on the
social role that lies play among the people at the center of her study.
Hurston describes two types of lies that were told by her interlocutors,
black residents of Eatonville, Florida. One type includes folktales that
are recounted among community members—mythical stories designed
to transmit cultural knowledge and mores. The other includes tales that
are told to nosy intruders—a sort of smoke screen intended to protect

marginalized black people from the prying gaze of the white world beyond. "We smile and tell him or her something that satisfies the white person," she writes, "because, knowing so little about us, he doesn't know what he is missing" (1990:2).

Hurston suggests that what Eatonvillians offer to outsiders in these contexts is not intimate insight into their community, its structure, organization, or values, but rather a fabricated story that sounds plausible, but is in fact only a mirrored reflection of the expectations the outsiders brought with them in the first place. Hurston's exploration of this subtle and contentious relationship between a guarded African American community and the always-inquiring white researchers is important. It is a vivid example of how knowledge is always positioned. Since such knowledge—historical or otherwise—is inevitably exchanged in a social interaction, the unique social dynamics that shape such interactions determine not only how knowledge is framed but, indeed, its very content.

Seventy years and four states away, the social dynamics between Union's descendant residents and the nosy outsiders preparing the NRHP nomination papers seem to be not very different from those described by Hurston in Eatonville. Although (contrary to Eatonville) Union has been home to both black and white residents, the process of gaining recognition as a historically black community reified a racial chasm engendered by 200 years of race-based slavery and nurtured by one-and-a-half centuries of social and legal segregation. In the previous chapter I highlighted how producing an official history of Union prevented black residents from recounting history on their own terms. Constrained within the framework of bureaucratic discourse about "historic significance," Union's history brokers elicited narratives that conformed to their own expectations of what a historic account should look like—and descendent residents obliged.

It was perhaps easy to miss that this was only a partial repertoire of narratives because descendant residents were proficient at producing histories that mirrored researchers' (including my own) expectations. As I describe in this chapter, the information that descendant residents offered to history brokers—place names, dates, names of key actors—correlated perfectly with the information the brokers were already gleaning from written records. Among themselves descendant residents shared histories that sounded nothing like the official history being written for the nomination papers—but history brokers never had a chance to learn those histories because, to borrow from Hurston, knowing so little about descendant residents, they simply did not know what they were missing.

Like Eatonville's residents in the 1930s, descendant residents contributed to Union's official history with narratives that reflected researchers' preconceived notions. And while researchers were busy "discovering" Union's African American history and using the oral histories to enhance the written record, descendants continued telling histories among themselves that spoke of a relationship to the past that is entirely absent in the official narrative. Indeed, the voices of Union's descendant residents were being silenced at the very moment that a history about them was being produced.

When I first arrived in Union, I, too, had the role of an outside researcher and the histories I recorded sounded very much like the histories recorded by the researchers who had worked on the historic nomination. Here is an example of some notes I jotted down in May 2000, when I first started working as an intern on the Union archiving project (I am "MB," while "LR" refers to one of my fellow researchers):

LR & MB met with Ms. Peters at her house and drove over to the former Maury home at Cedar Hill plantation. Hiked up to where the house had burned down in February 1935 (36?). Walked around the ruins and continued to the Maury family cemetery located behind the house. LF & MB walked around the heavily overgrown cemetery, cleared off James W. Maury and Mary (Brown) Maury gravestones, and copied down the inscriptions from approximately 8 of the gravestones. Returned to Ms. Peter's house and talked some more. Ms. Peters has many old papers from her father, who was also from Union, which she is willing to share with us. These papers include a deed for the land Ms. Peters lives on today. The

land had been part of the Cedar Hill plantation and the deed was signed
by some of the older residents of the area.

Over the years, perhaps because I returned to Union not as a historian
(and also because I had eventually become such a permanent fixture in
residents' homes), I began hearing histories told in a new way. Instead
of asking residents to discuss the topics I wanted to learn about, and
"harvesting" (the expression I sometimes heard historians use) residents'
stories for the facts that I considered relevant, I learned to shut up and
allow residents to teach me how they made sense of and conjured history when they were not "performing" for outside researchers. In fact, I
am not sure when residents first began including me in informal history
telling because at first I was not even aware that I was being told histories
at all. When I first arrived in Union my historical "radar" was trained
to pick up on the kinds of narratives that I would have registered as history (as in the example above, the year the plantation burned, people's
full legal names, inscriptions on gravestones), but descendant residents
offered historical narratives that for some time slipped by me without
my recognizing it.

In informal contexts, descendant residents would frequently narrate
histories as fragments embedded in discussions about other topics. My
field notes are filled with information about conversations I had with
residents, notes that at the time I thought were quite detailed. Here is an
example of notes I recorded in February 2002, after a visit to Ms. Celie
on the occasion of her 91st birthday:

> Ms. Celie said her son and daughter came to visit (from Washington DC)
> over the weekend to celebrate her birthday, but she told everyone else not
> to bother coming because it's too cold. She said people should come in
> the summer when they have time off and the weather is better so they can
> have a cookout for her birthday. . . .
>   Ms. Celie is incredibly active and very impressive. She lives on her own,
> takes care of her house, and does everything around the house herself.

While we sat in her living room, her granddaughter told me she came to visit Ms. Celie one day and the furniture was all moved around. She asked her grandma what she was doing and Ms. Celie answered nonchalantly that she was painting the walls and had to get behind the furniture. She couldn't do just a half-decent job—she had to go and paint behind the furniture, so she moved it all herself.

Ms. Celie's daughter laughed and added that one day she came over and found her mother on the roof. Ms. Celie was busy doing something (fixing shingles?). We all laughed. Ms. Celie responded, "Oh, that was nothing. It was the low side of the roof anyway, it was no big deal."

Historical knowledge was rarely the focus of our conversations, and yet, somehow, I realized one day that I knew a lot about residents' pasts and was familiar with various residents' particular historical repertoires. How did this happen? In taking notes about my time in Union and conversations with residents, I would record as much as I could remember based on the main topics we had discussed. I recorded intonations, I recorded asides and tangents. . . . But inevitably the conversations were far more nuanced than my notes could reveal, and interlaced among them were fragments of histories, inconspicuously enriching the conversation almost without my realizing it. The following is an excerpt of field notes from a visit with Jim Gaines in March 2002:

Today Mr. Gaines told me that the school closed because they didn't have enough kids going there. We were talking about racism and I told him that I was thinking about driving down to Florida but was nervous about getting pulled over. Mr. Gaines said "you never know. Sometimes they pull you over for no reason at all. They'll make something up."

Mieka: Yeah, people say things are all better today, but there is a lot of stuff that still goes on.

Mr. Gaines: You never know. . . . It depends on the person. It depends on the county. I never got a ticket outside of the state—all the tickets I've ever gotten were in state. I try to keep all the laws while I'm out of state because you never know what the place is like. Sometimes you still get pulled over for no reason and you don't know when it's going to happen.

At first, fragments were too obscure for me to notice—a remark made by a resident would have gone uncommented (and unrecorded) by me because I didn't have a frame of reference for it. Over time, as I became familiar with the histories that descendant residents told, the references became more visible to me . . . but by this time they seemed so obvious and repetitive that I did not bother to make note of them either in my field notes.

Histories in Union are embedded in discussions about the present, and repeated in different contexts. Inevitably, each repetition is slightly different, highlighting particular aspects of a person or event depending on the context within which the history is being told. This kind of historical transmission produces "thick" histories (to borrow Geertz's [1973] term)—three-dimensional and dynamic narratives that are continually produced, are patently conscious of their relationship to the present, and affirm a shared sense of community among the speakers.

Many of the histories I learned from descendant residents were told during conversations that focused on other issues: helping clean someone's living room, being schooled in the illusive art of garden keeping, taught to prepare dandelion wine, or otherwise engaged in some activity. Because of my age (younger than most of those with whom I spent time), relative lack of experience (in activities that many residents considered second nature, like gardening or animal husbandry), and tenuous social connections (not being a longtime Union resident or family member), I was almost always the lowest-status participant in these events. But my constant presence, and especially my friendship with Jim Gaines, somehow allowed my status to blur from being simply an outsider to becoming a sort of child-like person. I was constantly learning the proper things to say and do in different circumstances, so that it was appropriate for others to school me or socialize me in one practice or another. Even the faux pas that I inevitably made—like unthinkingly saying that the homemade dandelion wine "tastes like a wine cooler"—became opportunities for elder residents to teach me about any number of issues, and quite frequently through invocations of the past.

"What do you know about wine coolers?" Bill Anderson laughed, surprised. I wanted to swallow my tongue when I realized I was talking about a cheap alcoholic beverage to a man who I knew was a devout Christian. In church I learned that no consumption of alcohol is really acceptable, but cheap and relatively potent beverages that are readily available at the local supermarkets and associated with illicit lifestyles are especially stigmatized. I looked at Mr. Anderson and blushed, but he was still laughing when he repeated his question. "What do you know about that?" "Oh, nothing . . . ," I said in a fake innocent tone. "Well, the way you talk about it sounds like you tasted it," he demanded. "No, I never had it in my whole entire life," I exaggerated on purpose, indexing in my tone that this was a lie. "Well you're lying now," he retorted. "If you hear people talk about it you might know what they say about it, but you wouldn't know what it tastes like."

Instead of being scolding or disapproving—as I dreaded—Mr. Anderson mocked me openly, but was also understanding. "That's alright," he said. "We all do stuff we're not supposed to. The Bible says, 'all sin and come short of the glory of God.' If I sit around and tell you that I never did anything, that would mean I'm making God out to be a liar—and I wouldn't do that." Until this conversation my relationship with Mr. Anderson was cordial but also slightly distant. Something about this exchange created a change in both of us. We each found out something about the other's past that as mere acquaintances we were not supposed to know. Mr. Anderson eyed me up and down, humphed with a faint smile, and signaled for me to follow him to the porch on the other side of the house. As we walked together he muttered, "Because if you'd said you knew what the stuff *smelled* like, that would be one thing. But you said it *tasted* like a cooler. So yeah, you must know something about wine coolers."

We were done stirring our dandelion wine-in-the-making, so we walked over to a different part of the yard, plopped ourselves on two plastic chairs overlooking the railroad tracks, and talked about every-thing from gardening to grant writing, Israel to Korea, the Internet to the World Trade Center. Inevitably, Mr. Anderson peppered his conversation with stories about the past—both his own experiences and those of other people living in and around Union. There were a few stories that I knew about vaguely from the interviews I had conducted as an intern early in my fieldwork, but for the most part the stories that he shared with me on the back porch of the house I was hearing for the first time. These stories would have been insignificant in the official NRHP narrative, but they were significant in the lives of Union's descendent residents.

Over time, I came to distinguish between two, quite distinct types of historical exchanges that I would have with descendant residents. In formal interview settings, residents' historical narratives mirrored the kinds of exchanges they have learned to expect of academic researchers: exchanges in which the narrators are always the object of investigation but never themselves narrators of that history. Apart from interviews, however, historical knowledge is continuously shared on very different terms. In these exchanges, histories are never told as complete narratives, but as fragments repeated by different speakers in different contexts. The fragmented nature of the narratives meant that outsiders did not in fact have access to these histories (as I did not at first), so they were unable to recognize the inferences that were being made during the conversation. In a very real sense, such historical transmission defined quite clearly who was—and who was not—part of the community.

I began to grow familiar with some of the histories that residents told about people and places in Union, but these histories were rarely told as complete narratives in Labov's sense of the term (Labov and Waletsky 1967). Frequently I would hear part of a story on one day and a differ-ent part on another day—a different aspect or angle, different details, another dimension to the story. Some histories were told to me enough times and with enough variation that I could produce my own version (indeed my own history) of the events. Others I heard only once or twice, and I didn't accumulate enough fragments to get a sense of the event as a whole or have my own interpretation of it—though they did serve to elucidate whatever topic we might have been talking about at the time.

In Union, histories are not narrated as contained events that are (or even could be) recounted in full. Instead, histories are embedded in conversations about other contemporary issues, adding meaning, shedding light on, and enriching interlocutors' understanding of the present. The longer I spent in Union and the closer I became to some of the residents, the more iterations I was able to identify as narrations of the same events. And with the growing intimacy, so too the narratives themselves seemed to be transformed in focus and context, and my own ability to glean multiple layers of meaning from the narrative act itself grew. While this mode of historical transmission may not seem particularly unusual (indeed, descendent residents would confirm that they are not unusual), these narratives did not lay claim to "historic-ness," and as such were distinctly different from the kinds of narratives that the history brokers were producing.

With a general outline of Union's history already recorded in the NRHP nomination papers, an astute historian could cull information from the narratives told by descendent residents to add some colorful real-life anecdotes to what might otherwise be a flat narrative about Union. Where the nomination papers draw on historical documents to record the presence of a general merchandise store, for example, and identify the names of its owners, descendant residents could flesh out the story with memories about five-cent gingersnaps that could "nearly break your teeth" or about the owner, who doubled as an American Automobile Association agent and refused to sell policies to African Americans. While the NRHP narrative draws on written records to suggest that the period between 1930 and 1948 was Union's "decline" (evidenced by store closings, discontinued train service, and increasing accessibility to nearby Riverton), residents portrayed this period as marked by greater access to a social world beyond Union (thanks to an improved road system) and a vibrant social life within the community (including house parties, active social clubs, community-wide sporting events, and an always dynamic church body) that flourished despite—perhaps even because of—changing economic conditions.

The stories that residents narrate about their past may perhaps seem unremarkable to outsiders seeking historic narratives that "say something about something"—a story about playing horseshoes, for example, may not seem as interesting or exciting as one about black troops enlisted during the Second World War (as described below), but these were the histories that descendant residents conjured and shared when they were not being summoned to produce data in the service of others' interests.

But the histories that residents narrate among themselves offer more than just colorful anecdotes or quaint but prosaic memories. They reveal a unique relationship to history and the past that is entirely absent from the official NRHP narrative. An "anticipated" reading of residents' histories might corroborate that they correlate with the history recorded in the NRHP nomination papers. But such a reading could obscure the perspective that residents offer about the roles of history and the past in their own lives. It is the historian's creation, an imposition of the data onto the editor's own interests and perspectives, not a narrative produced by the descendant residents themselves. "Recovering" historical anecdotes about Union might masquerade as an indigenous artifact (a fusion of stories told in the residents' own words), but this would, in fact, be an ethnographic invention.

Instead, I would like to suggest an "unanticipated" approach to these narratives. Rather than scouring the histories told during informal settings for facts that link them to the grand-narrative history—facts that prove, disprove, flesh out, or complicate the story told in the NRHP papers (this would be an "anticipated" reading)—my goal in this chapter is to highlight how histories operate in descendant residents' own lives, allowing their meanings to emerge in a way that is not available in the NRHP papers. The memories that descendant residents consider worth keeping and the contexts in which the narratives are shared provide insight into how residents think about history and the past.

A growing body of literature has emerged focused on identifying and articulating the hidden histories (Schneider and Rapp 1995) of those whose lives are "under the radar" of mainstream historical investigation. Though this scholarship is relatively interdisciplinary, most contributions inevitably come from the field of history, which has been recovering the lives and experiences of so-called marginalized historical subjects—African Americans, women, peasants, colonial subjects, etc. (A review of such "new social history" can be found in Appleby et al. 1994, and Molho and Wood 1998. For African American history, see also Higginbotham 1992.) Anthropologists have contributed to this oeuvre by exposing ways of remembering and inscribing memories that are not always evident to a Western readership (e.g., Rosaldo 1980; Sahlins 1981, 1985; Wolf 1982; Alonso 1988; Stewart 1996; Borofsky 2000; Price 2002; Shaw 2002). This literature demonstrates that histories persist and can be reconstructed even in cultural contexts where they might initially seem to be absent.

This chapter builds on the evocative insights offered by the existing literature, but takes a slightly different course of investigation. In exposing hidden histories, scholarship tends to eclipse the possibility that a certain community might not be narrating histories (hidden or in plain view) at all. Instead of uncovering existing histories, then, I concentrate on the contexts in which the past is invoked and the meanings assigned by Union residents to these invocations. I do not mean to imply that Union's descendant residents are somehow "without" history, but to suggest that the assumption that it must exist may prevent us from learning other ways of relating to the past. Instead of asking "How are histories narrated?" I am interested in the question "When and how is the past invoked?" Asking the question in this manner allows me to include invocations of the past, including those that do not register as historical narratives.

Union's descendant residents produce histories that look and act differently from those produced in the NRHP narrative or by Union's history brokers. Descendant residents are certainly capable of engaging historians (including, initially, me) who want to know about their lives and experiences: the narratives descendants offer in these formal contexts might be thought of as "flat" histories, while the narratives they produce in informal contexts with people whom they consider part of their community might be thought of as "thick" histories.

The previous chapter focused on the history brokers' histories of Union which, I argued, linked stories about specific events to narratives about broad historical processes. History brokers' histories organize these stories into a chronology, highlighting events that enrich the listener's (or reader's) understanding of social, political, and economic life during a particular era. Descendant residents' histories, on the other hand, do none of the above. Instead of focusing on chronology, descendants' histories highlight aspects of particular events that elucidate something about the present. The past is narrated based on its ability to offer insight into, teach a lesson about, or provide a context for contemporary social, political, and economic situations.

While history brokers connect stories from Union to a national official history, descendant residents narrate histories as a way to instruct listeners (and perhaps the narrator as well) about appropriate and inappropriate social responses to particular situations. History becomes a resource for knowing how to make sense of the present (now is better than then / then is better than now / then offers an example of a similar situation and some possible outcomes / then teaches us about human nature / then prepares us for what life might bring). The sections that follow provide examples of how the past is conjured by descendent residents, and offers an analysis of some of the ways the past is engaged in everyday discourse and activities—the forms that histories take and the social function they fulfill.

Thick Narratives: Histories

I first began to notice the different roles histories play in the lives of Union's descendant residents as I transitioned from my role as a historian sent to collect oral histories for the Union archive to that of an ethnographer spending qualitative time with residents beyond our formal interviews. After interacting with residents for more than a year, gathering "knowledge" through the oral history interviews about the lives and experiences of Union's African American residents, as an ethnographer I spent more casual and unstructured time there, participating in a variety of activities and discussing with residents a far greater range of topics than I had before. Of course I was still interested in residents' relationship to history and the past, but I also took part in unrelated experiences and conversation topics, as happens in ethnographic fieldwork, and in long-lasting social relationships in general.

As we learned about each other's lives, experiences, and interests, some of the same stories I had recorded early in my fieldwork were being told to me again in more casual circumstances. At first I wondered whether my interlocutors forgot that they had already shared with me a narrative about a particular story, but I remained attentive and realized that although I might already have known about some of the events being recounted, both the format and contents of the histories shifted when recounted in casual conversations. With each retelling, the narratives would take on a slightly different form, depending on the particular point or observation being made between the history and the topic of conversation.

Deliberate History (Jim Gaines)

On one occasion, Jim Gaines related two very different versions of the same narrative within the course of one afternoon. We were sitting in the enclosed porch of his home on a still chilly day in early April, poring over a small folding table as I tried to teach him a card game. Mr. Gaines was homebound, and I thought he might enjoy knowing some games that he could play when no one else was around. He paid attention as I flipped and organized the cards spread before us, explaining the rules for a game of solitaire. He followed my explanations as small stacks of ascending- and descending-order cards began forming on the table, but I could tell he was only half-interested.

"We used to play horseshoes," Mr. Gaines told me, still looking at the cards as the memory surfaced. "I still have some," he noted, gesturing out to the yard, "hanging from the tree." He pointed to the large tree in front of the house and told me there were horseshoes hanging there. Not sure whether or not I could see them, he directed me to go and take a closer look. I walked out to the tree and saw two large horseshoes hanging from a nail wedged about halfway up the trunk. "What are they for?" I asked when I came back into the house.

MR. GAINES: They've never been used, though.
MIEKA: But what are they supposed to be for?
MR. GAINES: Playing. They were never on a horse. Too big.

Mr. Gaines explained that there were different kinds of horseshoes— those designed to be used on horses, and others that were "raised especially for playing."

MR. GAINES: The ones for playing are much bigger. Made it a little easier to play that way. The ones hanging on the tree are for playing, they ain't for no horses.
MIEKA: Yeah, they are pretty big.
MR. GAINES: They wouldn't fit a horse.
MIEKA: Maybe a big horse?
MR. GAINES: Maybe like a Belgian or a Clydesdale.
MIEKA: Maybe so. Did you ever play?
MR. GAINES: Sure I did! We used to play horseshoes. We'd go to Washington Park.
MIEKA: You mean in Riverton?
MR. GAINES: Yeah. [He mentions two or three names of people he used to play with.] You have a peg, you drive it into the ground. You throw the horseshoe. If it hits the peg and wraps around it, that's five points.
MIEKA: Wraps around it? What's that?

MR. GAINES: (holding his hands up to demonstrate) If it spins around the peg.

MIEKA: (clearly a novice to the game) How many points do you get if it actually goes on the peg?

MR. GAINES: That is when it goes on to the peg. If it spins around and around, that means it went on.

MIEKA: Oh. But what if it spins around and flies off?

MR. GAINES: No. You don't get points for that. Just if it spins around and stays. That was five points.

Appreciating Mr. Gaines's vivid memory of playing horseshoes, it occurred to me it could be nice to have this story recorded on tape. I asked him if it would be OK if I recorded the conversation and, when he agreed, went to get my recording equipment from the car. In less than two minutes I was back in the house, set up, and looking forward to picking up the conversation we had left off. But with the tape recorder on, the tone and contents of the narrative changed. While earlier the conversation evolved as a light-hearted exchange with a quick series of questions and answers, the recorded version was much more deliberate. And while the first version hinged on Mr. Gaines's personal engagement with the game, explaining the rules, and sprinkling the technical information with tidbits about the places where he played and the people who participated, the recorded version focused entirely on the names of the people who played the game:

MR. GAINES: Yeah, Eddie Wilkins used to play all the time. Eddie Wilkins. The only one I know

MIEKA: Eddie who?

MR. GAINES: Wilkins.

MIEKA: Wilkins.

MR. GAINES: Wilkins. W-I-L-K-I-N-S. Eddie Wilkins. He used to live on Chester Avenue. He's dead now, though.

(PAUSE)

MIEKA: He taught you how to play?

MR. GAINES (LOST IN THOUGHT): Huh?

MIEKA: He taught you how to play horseshoes?

MR. GAINES: Nooo . . . heck, no. I was taught . . . ever since I worked on the farm. I'll tell you when I first started: [It was] back in the—oh, Lord . . . back in the thirties, honey.

MIEKA: That's when you started playing it?

MR. GAINES: The Thirties. Yes, Lord. When [Union Road] was a sand/clay road.

As soon as he completed telling this history, Mr. Gaines returned to his normal tempo and timbre, and the conversation regained its easygoing pace and usual rapid change of topics. We talked about the sand/clay road and about one of the nearby churches. He told me a bit about a local all-black battalion during the Second World War, and we ended with a conversation about agricultural technology and some of the techniques employed when he used to work as a young man in a nearby farm. But I wanted to record more about the horseshoe game in particular so, during a lull in the conversation, I asked (in a somewhat formal tone) that we return to the original topic.

MIEKA: So you want to tell me about the horseshoes?

MR. GAINES: I can't tell you nothing. I don't remember nobody that played horseshoes. See, all them people are dead.

MIEKA: Mm.

MR. GAINES: But Eddy Wilkins was the one that used to have the horseshoe contest. We used to play horseshoes on the holidays.

MIEKA: Oh, OK.

MR. GAINES: See, but that was the only one that I know living. I don't remember the guys who played with them.

MIEKA: But just tell me the thing that you told me before I got the tape recorder. About how you play it.

MR. GAINES: Oh! You drive a wooden peg in the ground.

MIEKA: OK.

MR. GAINES: About 18 inches long.

ME: Uh-huh.

MR. GAINES: Down to about 12 inches.

ME: That's how far you drive it down.

ME: OK.

MR. GAINES: Put in the horseshoe and hit it [so it goes] around.

ME: Mm-hm.

Mr. Gaines's replies grant insight into the difference between the ways formal and informal histories are narrated in Union. In the first conversation I had with him, the game of horseshoes came up organically; the second time it was elicited. In both cases Mr. Gaines was conveying information that was "accurate," but the two exchanges sound and feel—and act—differently in a social context. By the time of this interview, Mr. Gaines and I had already spent a lot of time together and established a comfortable rapport with one another. The original history that he narrated, therefore, was an informal recounting of the experience of playing horseshoes. In the recorded versions the narrative is far more descriptive. Both times (when I first turned on the tape recorder and asked that he tell me about playing horseshoes, and later when I requested that we return to the topic), Mr. Gaines shifts to a more deliberate tone, and refocuses the narrative from the experience of the game to a record of facts—stake size, players' names, etc., noting the name of one player and explaining that he is unable to give me more—presumably because the other people are dead. While telling history in a casual conversation produced a vivid and elaborated description of the game, recording history on tape yielded a much more static and flat description.

Articulating two such distinct narratives, Mr. Gaines compels us to recognize the distinction he makes between formal and informal historical narration. While the first version of the story in the casual exchange was told about a personal experience, the second version is a carefully crafted and deliberate narrative that aims to produce accurate records of people, places, and events. The first version was lighthearted, the second solemn and composed. The first version was formed through a succession of questions and answers; the second concluded after only one or two sentences. The first version was open-ended and ongoing, the second finite. Mr. Gaines had a good understanding of what formal histories are supposed to look like—and that image did not include open-ended chatter about his own personal experiences of an enjoyable game.[1]

"My Memory Is Terrible" (Celia Marshall)

I had had similar encounters with history telling among other descendant residents as well. Early in my ethnographic fieldwork, after avoiding me during my first two summers of interviews, I finally had the opportunity to meet and interview Celia Marshall. Ms. Celie (as most people referred to her) was born in 1911, making her the oldest resident in Union, and had lived on the same property her entire life. I had hoped to interview her for the Union Archive when I first began working in Union, but since she seemed reluctant to meet me, I respected her feelings and interviewed other residents instead.

Ms. Celie's granddaughter, however, had different ideas. Knowing that her grandmother was hesitant about meeting strangers, but wanting her memories to be recorded, Louise tricked both of us into meeting. Early in November Louise told her grandmother that she was coming by to visit "with a friend." She told me that she had convinced her grandmother to do the interview. In truth, Louise and several other family members knew I was conducting oral history interviews with other residents and conspired to get their matriarch involved despite her hesitance. Neither Ms. Celie nor I realized we had been duped when I arrived at her home with Louise that Saturday afternoon.

I was introduced to Ms. Celie and several family members who were in the living room awaiting our arrival: her son and daughter, visiting from Washington, D.C., and a grandson who lives in Union. The living room was lined with photos of family members—numbering easily more than a hundred. Children, grandchildren, great-grandchildren, and great-great-grandchildren peered at us from every corner of the room; even the piano keyboard was covered with photographs and photo albums. "It's like being surrounded by your family!" I remarked. "Yes, it is," she replied, smiling and scanning the framed faces around us.

I settled in and pulled out my tape recorder and notepad, asking Ms. Celie if it would be alright if I interviewed her. Before she could protest, her son and daughter agreed on her behalf and egged their mother on to tell me about her life. "Tell her about what you remember, Mama," her daughter said. Her son and grandchildren agreed. Ms. Celie looked around at each of us and sighed aloud. "I don't remember," she said. I still hadn't picked up on what had happened, but felt awkward, recognizing her reluctance. "You don't have to if you don't want to," I apologized, but Louise quickly jumped in. "Grandmama, this is the girl I've been telling you about from the university. She wants to do a history of Union. Just tell her what you remember. You don't have to remember everything." She turned to me and explained, "She's afraid she's gonna forget something." Ms. Celie sighed again and agreed to do the interview. I had barely enough time to ask Celie for her full name before the rest of the family chimed in. "Tell her about the school," Louise suggested.

MS. CELIE: My teacher's name was Alice Cummings, Reverend Cummings' wife. She taught . . . I think she did. Did she teach there? Or did. . . . Or she taught in that little school. I can't remember. Because remember— they built a little house right on the church ground. It used to be down on the church ground and that was . . . I went to the first school for a while, but I can't. I tell you, my memory, honey, I don't know . . . I can't do you any good at all!

MIEKA: That's OK.

MS. CELIE: Because my . . . (laughs) my memory is terrible!

GRANDDAUGHTER: Just give her a little bit and she's going to look it up. She can find it. She found a lot of it on the computer.

Like Mr. Gaines's description of the horseshoe game, Ms. Celie began by listing the names of people she remembered and describing the location of the school. Once she depleted her memory of this sort of knowledge, she apologized for not being able to offer more. In the end, the communal interview lasted for almost two hours. I asked some of the questions, which Ms. Celie and her family answered, and her family members asked more questions, which she and the other members would answer. When she offered repeated apologies for not being able to remember, her children would interrupt and complete the stories.

I learned, eventually, that her initial reticence stemmed from her reluctance to have strangers come to her house, combined with the feeling that she could not offer the kinds of historical narrations she assumed I would be interested in. But, as with Mr. Gaines, I found that in informal contexts Ms. Celie was ever ready to share histories with others, as well as, eventually, me. Over the years, I came to spend a significant amount of time at her home, and began learning her own repertoire of histories that she shared with family and friends.

This initial meeting was the first and last formal interview I conducted with her, but in everyday conversations or family gatherings, Ms. Celie regularly shared stories about her life and Union in general. The histories she shared included stories about the many years she worked as a domestic on a nearby "plantation"; walking her eight children to the store where they would catch the school bus—then continuing along the railroad track to get to work; growing enough vegetables to feed her large family, and the tiredness she felt after staying up all night canning. Even if she did not remember everything she hoped to of the more than nine decades she had been alive, each of her historical narratives relayed vivid memories of the experiences she had—including events that took place early in her life.

On an especially pleasant March afternoon, I checked in to see whether Ms. Celie had started her garden for the spring. She was indoors, and we watched a little television as we chatted about this and that. Returning to a favorite topic—how children today act "wild" compared to when she was growing up—she told me that she believed today's children were not being disciplined properly:

> MIEKA: I know what you mean. If you smack a kid today you can get sued . . .
>
> MS. CELIE: (laughs) Oh boy. I can remember my grandmother now. All she had to do is wince her nose and I knew it was coming. And there was nothing I could do about it! Yeah, my grandmother. . . . Golly gee, she used to discipline us. (we laugh) I remember her now, looking at that picture. . . . (she gestures over to a picture on the table—a photo of an 11-year old Celie standing beside her cousin and grandmother) Yup. That's how it was back then. These days you don't do that anymore.

I was a little surprised at the ease with which she was drawing on these memories. I recalled how, during our original interview, she had discussed memories of her grandmother with significant hesitation. Here is how the exchange took place during the original interview:

> MIEKA: When you were growing up you used to go with your mom to work?
>
> MS. CELIE: Yeah.
>
> MIEKA: What did you do the rest of the day?
>
> MS. CELIE: Oh, well—came back home and . . .
>
> DAUGHTER: And grandma.
>
> MS. CELIE: Huh?
>
> DAUGHTER: Grandma.
>
> MS. CELIE: Yeah, my grandmother was there when I came back home.
>
> MIEKA: Your grandmother lived with you?
>
> MS. CELIE: My grandmother lived over—yeah. She lived over at my uncle's [where Celie also lived]. She stayed in the house. Of course, she took care of his children when they were small.

Ms. Celie's daughter, who had heard many stories about the grand-mother, wanted her mother to infuse the narrative with memories of her. Ms. Celie obliged, noting that her grandmother "was there when I came back home," and "she took care of [the uncle's] children." Speaking to a stranger who was taking down a formal history, she chose a format she felt appropriate, one that includes descriptive facts rather than expe-riential memories. The examples are parallel in that each invokes the grandmother's parenting practices, and yet in the casual conversation she narrates an intimate aspect of their relationship ("All she had to do is wince her nose and I knew it was coming"), while in the formal interview she narrates a description of the grandmother's social roles ("She stayed in the house" and "she took care of his children").

In these two different kinds of contexts, Union's descendant residents assert the format and content they consider appropriate for formal his-tory, and, on the other hand, the format and content appropriate for casual exchanges of historical knowledge. Although in casual settings residents narrate a wide variety of histories, the histories told in formal contexts are stripped of their experiential contents. In the following sec-tion I draw on narratives that were shared with me during the ethno-graphic portion of my fieldwork, after I had already known the residents and developed a relationship with them over the course of nearly two years.

Thick Narratives: Talking about the Past

In a small community like Union, where residents have intimate knowledge of the ins and outs of each other's lives, narrating the past often evolves as an open-ended and ongoing exchange. When invoking past events in conver-sations with other members of the community, narrators can be relatively assured that their interlocutors have some context for the events or expe-riences described, or the social relationships alluded to in the narrative. Many of Union's descendant residents grew up knowing each other, attend-ing the same church, their families socializing together some also working alongside each other. Over the generations, members of some of the larger families (including the Marshalls, the Farradays, and the Gaineses) also became related to one another through marriage and adoptive kinship.[2]

Community members hearing a narrative about a particular event were likely to have already heard about the event from someone else or the same narrator, or even witnessed it themselves—and they might know some or all of the people involved. In comparison with formal histories, then—which are narrated as objective descriptions of past people, places, and events—informal histories fill a different semiological and social role, and are themselves enriched by the social contexts in which they are invoked.

Repetition (House Fire/William Anderson and Jim Gaines)

In informal contexts, the same story might be repeated, each narration shedding light on different social phenomena according to the context within which it was invoked. New angles to the story are revealed with each retelling, details not mentioned earlier are emphasized in subsequent renditions, while other details are dropped. The result yields "piled up structures of inference and implication" and "thick" insights into the experiences being narrated (Geertz 1973:7). Such density was not offered—and could not be captured—during formal interviews, nor could it easily be relayed in the formal NRHP narratives. Each new rendition of the informal histories, then, is not intended to transmit some sort of objective historical knowledge, but to reveal new dimensions of and insights into already-known circumstances, to share an evolving perspective on social life as a whole through invocation and reexamination of past experiences, to deepen social relations between narrators and their interlocutors, and to expand an understanding of present situations through lessons learned in the past.

Discussing the frequency with which house fires once used to occur, Mr. Anderson told me about several houses that he remembered burning down.

MIEKA: I know Mr. Gaines's house burned down, too.

MR. ANDERSON: Yeah. . . . That was terrible. I remember when it happened. It was snowing. Mr. Gaines's wife and my wife both worked together. Jim carried his wife to work, and I carried my wife to work, and Jim was supposed to carry both of them back in the morning, but I got a call in the middle of the night—"Come quick! William, get up! Jim Gaines's house caught on fire!" By the time we got there it was completely burned down. And it was all snow on the ground.

MIEKA: What happened?

MR. ANDERSON: The place burned down because it was a wood frame.

MIEKA: What did Mr. Gaines do?

MR. ANDERSON: He had a cousin who lived down the road. He went and stayed there. They had kids, too, and they all went to stay with them. That's when they built that little structure behind the house.

MIEKA: You mean that long thing?

MR. ANDERSON: The one that's behind the house. Yeah, they built that thing up right quick. They built it up in two or three days.

Although the exchange begins with my saying that I knew about the incident, Mr. Anderson offers to narrate this history to me—not to educate me about what happened, but to share his experience of the event, a perspective I had not yet been offered. On other occasions Mr. Anderson told me this story again, with different points being emphasized. Sometimes it was about the wives—Ms. Gaines and Ms. Anderson—who were working late that night at the hospital and came home to a pile of ashes. Sometimes it was a way to illustrate how the community banded together to help build a new home for the Gaines family. Other residents mentioned the particular fire on different occasions as well, each offering their own perspective on the event.

The details that narrators choose to emphasize in any given historical rendition vary according to the reason for telling the story in the first place. The burning house was also prominent, of course, in Mr. Gaines's own historical repertoire. The first time I heard him tell about this event was in a formal interview during one of our very first meetings. It offers an interesting rendition of the event both with regard to the experience of the fire, and to the subsequent financial transactions:

MR. GAINES: My wife had been shopping [for Christmas presents] for the children, and the other house didn't have no basement. But we had dug out and had a furnace under. It was a coal furnace. And she bought the stuff for Christmas, and I was mopping the floor—about three days before Christmas Eve. I told the children to go to bed. All went to bed. (pause) At the time we went to bed I heard something crackling in the wall. Like something scratching the wall—

MIEKA: Right . . .

MR. GAINES: And that was the fire. It was burning out but I didn't know. It was snow on the ground—about three-four inches deep, the wind blowing. . . . That other house burned down in about 45-50 minutes. Burned everything we had. I was the only one man to put the children out of the house—my wife was at work. She went crazy.

MIEKA: Wow.

MR. GAINES: [She] took it so hard—we didn't have nothing left.

MIEKA: What did you do?

MR. GAINES: Stayed over next door with my cousin over on the hill until we built that little bungalow right back there. (points at the one-story building next door) See that bungalow over there?

MIEKA: Oh, that's what you built?

MR. GAINES: Yeah, we built that and stayed in that house until we built this house.

MIEKA: Oh, wow.

MR. GAINES: We had a lot of people to help, a lot of friends.

MIEKA: Did anyone get hurt?

MR. GAINES: No, uh-uh. I got them out! I woke 'em, I woke up when I heard something. I don't sleep that hard. I could hear something crackle in the wall. . . . And it sounded like a mouse or a rat eating, but it was fire burning the inside. By the time that wind hit it—45 minutes and that house . . . I guess it had about five or six rooms burn up in about 45 minutes with nothing left. Well, we stayed next door and built our little house over there.

MIEKA: It was a wood house?

MR. GAINES: Yeah.

MIEKA: I see you built a brick one instead.

MR. GAINES: Yeah, yeah. But I got a lot of help. Thank God I had a lot of friends.

MIEKA: Yeah? Who helped?

MR. GAINES: I couldn't afford to build it now.

MIEKA: Oh, people actually came in and helped build it?

MR. GAINES: Lord, yes. Some of them didn't charge nothing—bricklayers.

MIEKA: No kidding.

MR. GAINES: See, I knew everybody back then. Four-five of the guys who came to the barbershop were bricklayers. Yeah, some of 'em didn't charge me nothing! Had two jobs and wouldn't take no money. People were real good to us.

At the time I conducted this interview, Mr. Gaines and I did not yet know each other very well, and Mr. Gaines sticks to a descriptive history that has a clear-cut beginning, middle, and end.[3] This history opens with an introduction to the event (Mama "had bought the stuff for Christmas" and it was "about three days before Christmas Eve"), describes the event itself, and ends with a coda depicting the social and economic ramifications of the fire. This is not the thick experiential history that I would come to hear Mr. Gaines narrate many times later. It was a simple, linear narrative.

Mr. Anderson's first history of the fire focuses predominantly on the night of the event—the conditions (wives at work, snow on the ground), and the tragedy of the fire itself. The second narrative notes the fire only inasmuch as it is a catalyst for understanding one facet of Mr. Gaines's apparent fiscal irresponsibility. Mr. Gaines's history, though it is factual rather than experiential, focuses less on the fire itself and more on what the fire meant: the Christmas gifts that were lost, the house that was gone ("burnt everything we had"), the new bungalow that had to be built, and the need to draw on social networks in order to have the new house built.

The more narratives one hears about the event (and almost all descendant residents shared some rendition of this particular house fire), the thicker one's insight into the experiential social world in which the event took place. "Every corner of space conceals a multitude of individuals each of whom totalizes the trend of history in a manner which cannot be compared to others," writes Lévi-Strauss. "A truly total history would cancel itself out" (1966:257). In telling multiple and slightly varying histories about the past, descendant residents do not create a "truly total history," but produce instead a far more complex, thick relationship to the past than any descriptive history could. Those who take part in these exchanges come to develop a three-dimensional relationship with the events being recounted.

In local and informal settings where narrators and their interlocutors are familiar with one another (and often also with the event being narrated), there is no need to produce a "complete" narrative that has a clear beginning, middle, or end. Histories are abbreviated, sometimes only a fraction of the event is described, with a resulting narrative that might not necessarily make sense to someone who is not already familiar with the story. At times, as in William Anderson's second history of the fire, only a short snippet is offered about the event itself, while the rest of the history is an exposition on the consequences, motivations, or implications of the event.

Other informal histories might be said to be "missing" one of the standard narrative components (orientation, complication, evaluation, resolution, and coda, according to Labov and Waletski 1967)—a practice that might suggest to an outsider that these narrators are not skilled storytellers. But Union's descendant residents are, in fact, quite skilled history tellers. The histories are perfectly legible to their intended audience, who know that the fragment they may be hearing in one conversation relates to other fragments that they may have heard in other conversations. As explained below, transmitting histories in informal settings is only seldom done for the sake of learning about the past. Much more frequently, histories are embedded into conversations about the present and intended for learning from the past: to elucidate some aspect of the topic at hand, and simultaneously to affirm a shared sense of community among the speakers.

Omitted Temporalities (Louise Coles and William Anderson)

I learned that even when histories were offered as "complete" narratives (according to the Labovian definition), narrators frequently did not mention the time period in which an event took place. Because the intended audience was usually familiar with a particular history (and therefore also when an event took place), temporal grounding was not necessary, nor was it particularly relevant. Temporality was often tangential to the central purpose of relating the narrative.

Union's descendant residents often shared with me histories that did not offer any timeframe at all. Occasionally I would learn with surprise that a story I was listening to that I assumed took place in the recent past (since the narrator did not specify otherwise) had, in fact, transpired decades ago. When timeframe was relevant to the reason for narrating the history (e.g., to illustrate how long the narrator had been involved in a particular activity, or to emphasize a difference between "now" and "then"), temporality was offered as part of the narrative. But if a different point was being made (e.g., to teach about human nature, to offer examples from similar situations), temporality became a tertiary detail or was left out completely. In contrast with the formal histories in which temporality is a critical component of the narrative, the point of history telling for descendent residents was not to produce a chronology, but to annotate the larger conversation within which the narrative was told.

Mr. Anderson's Sit-In

One day, as Mr. Anderson and I exchanged stories about frustrating work experiences, he mentioned to me that he worked as a plumber and

Jim Gaines, standing beside his car (ca. 1940s), Union, Virginia. Photo courtesy of Julia Peters.

maintenance man in a nearby housing project. "When you live in the projects you're not supposed to have babies," Mr. Anderson said off-handedly. "Really!" I responded, surprised at what seemed like some sort of civil rights violation. I assumed he was describing a present-day regulation. Mr. Anderson confirmed, "You're not supposed to. If you live in the projects, you can't have babies." "But what happens if you do?" I asked. "Where are you supposed to go?" To illustrate his point, he explained:

MR. ANDERSON: They don't really say where, you're just not supposed to be there. The girl lived [in the projects]. She had a baby and the people that work there found out about it, but they just said "don't do it again." They didn't do anything about it. Then she went ahead and got pregnant again, and I was supposed to pick up her stuff. She was supposed to get out by a certain time, and I was supposed to go in and get her stuff out—me and another guy. When it was time to go to the place, usually the way we did it, we would just go in, get all the stuff out, and be done in about half an hour. When we got there, there were people all over—a whole bunch of people came. They were black and white. They came in and sat on all the furniture in the house. There were people all over the place. It was so many of them that not all of them even fit inside the house.

MIEKA: What do you mean? They just came?

MR. ANDERSON: They were organized. It was some organization. They came and sat on the chairs and on the furniture, and when we came and tried to get the stuff. . . . You come up and say politely, "Please I'm trying to get this sofa. Can you please move from the sofa?" The guy was sitting on the sofa, just looked away, pretending he didn't hear you. He acted funny. He just look. (mimics the man looking in every direction except at Mr. Anderson) We couldn't move any of the furniture, so we didn't know what to do.

MIEKA: Really, they did that?

MR. ANDERSON: Yeah, it was a sit-in.

MIEKA: A sit-in??

MR. ANDERSON: Yeah.

Taken back by an expression that I associated with the civil rights movement of the 1950s and 1960s, I was thrown into confusion. In my own speech repertoire, I would have expected that a narrative about an event that transpired several decades ago would be framed in a way that indexed that I was now hearing a historical narrative. But Mr. Anderson did not offer such a frame. Unsure, I hedged:

MIEKA: When did this happen, Mr. Anderson?

MR. ANDERSON: Oh, it was a long time ago.

MIEKA: How long?

MR. ANDERSON: Maybe 30 or 40 years ago.

Excited by the connection to larger social processes—and especially to the civil rights movement, a pivotal moment in racial politics in the United States—I wanted to know more about what I considered to be a historic event that Mr. Anderson had encountered. But he was not trying to draw connections to larger social processes (he does not even mention the civil rights movement, though he does use the term "sit-in"). This history was not invoked for its own sake, but in the context of difficulties that he sometimes encountered on the job. In the exchange that followed, our different relationships to this event become apparent. I was interested in the story as an anecdotal example—a part of history with which I was familiar and that I cared about. Mr. Anderson shared it as an outstanding example of job-related difficulties.

MIEKA: Mr. Anderson, that was a sit-in!!

MR. ANDERSON: Yeah, they wouldn't move.

MIEKA: What did you think about it?

MR. ANDERSON: Well I just did what they told me to do. My job was to go in and move the person out, and that's what I was trying to do. But they weren't letting me do my job. There was police officers all over the place.

MIEKA: Police officers??

MR. ANDERSON: Yeah. Armed troops and everything.

MIEKA: What were they there for?

MR. ANDERSON: To protect.

MIEKA: Who?

MR. ANDERSON: Us! To protect me and the other guy while we did our job. We didn't know if it was going to turn violent or nothing.

MIEKA: But do you think that she should have been moved out?

MR. ANDERSON: She knew the rules. She knew that she wasn't supposed to have no babies, and she had the first one already and nobody said anything. Then she went ahead and got pregnant again even though she knew she wasn't supposed to.

MIEKA: So what was the outcome?

MR. ANDERSON: They won.

MIEKA: Who won?

MR. ANDERSON: The woman with the baby. She didn't have to move in the end. There was too much pressure and the police didn't like all the attention.

In this example, Mr. Anderson does not even shift to the past tense when he describes the events at the housing project: "You're not supposed to have babies," he explains, if you live in the projects. And even though my questions may have indicated that I was confused about the time frame of the story ("What happens if you do?" "Where are you supposed to go?"), they seem appropriate to Mr. Anderson.

Mr. Anderson's sit-in narrative was framed within a discussion that employed history as an anecdote, but the conversation was not itself about history. Although the event took place in the relatively distant past (he eventually mentioned it was "a long time ago"), in a period that history books often describe as pivotal in American history and in a social world that Mr. Anderson himself acknowledges is quite different from today, this history was shared as an example of work-related difficulties. The experience was eventful, to be sure (he still remembers it quite vividly some 40 years after the fact), but it is invoked as a perhaps unusual but nonetheless indicative example of the kinds of difficulties he encounters as an employee in public housing.

Significantly, in relating the event to me, the frustration that Mr. Anderson experienced during this event was apparent in both his posture and intonation. The transcript does not convey the emotion behind the words, but their delivery cannot hide the strong feelings that he has about this experience. "She knew the rules," he protests. "She went ahead and got pregnant again even though she knew she wasn't supposed to." While I was enthralled with what I perceived as the historic-ness of the moment and wanted to know the outcome, Mr. Anderson expressed his frustration at encountering this kind of situation.

Growing up and raising his family during socio-legal segregation, Mr. Anderson did what he could to ensure he passed under the radar of Jim Crow laws—whether it meant doing what was expected of him, "doing my job," or staying out of visible range altogether (by living in rural Union, for example, rather than the somewhat more urban Riverton, where he was born). "The girl," on the other hand, blatantly defied the rules and forced him to take sides. The police, he noted, "didn't like all the attention"—and frankly neither did Mr. Anderson. He offers his narrative not because it was part of larger social, political or economic trends, but because it conveys what the experience was like for him. It is a lesson in "the kinds of things that people do," it offers an example of job-related difficulties, and it offers evidence of his own work ethic and unyielding moral character.

Runaway Children (Louise Coles)

Although my own expectations of narratives (as the above example demonstrates) often were that events be introduced with what Labov and Waletsky call a temporal "orientation" (1967:32), it is clear that descendant residents frequently omitted what to them was an unnecessary detail. As I stood with Louise Coles in her kitchen and helped prepare lunch, we chatted about some of the people who lived in Union. I told Louise that I had seen one of her neighbors jogging a few days before. "He was a long way from his home," I said. "He must have really been running a lot." As the conversation evolved, Louise was reminded of runaway children who once found their way to Union—an event I later learned had taken place many years earlier, but that during this exchange I assumed had happened recently.

> LOUISE: Yeah, [the neighbor] used to run out here, too.
>
> MIEKA: Oh yeah? On this road?
>
> LOUISE: On the railroad tracks.
>
> MIEKA: That's kinda scary. What if the train comes?
>
> LOUISE: He just goes between the tracks. You could get fined for it—but I don't know, with all those hobos running around on the tracks I don't know why they care about these people.

MIEKA: Oh really? There's hobos around here?

LOUISE: Oh yeah, sometimes. One time there were these runaway kids
that came over on the train. They had come all the way down from
upstate Virginia and got off right next to my grandmother's house
because the girl cut her foot.

MIEKA: Man. How many kids was it?

LOUISE: It was three kids. The oldest about 14, but the 13-year-old girl cut
her foot and she was sitting right next to the railroad track. They
were shivering and freezing, and they were cold and hungry. The boy
went over to my grandmother's house and asked if he could have a
sandwich. Grandma gave him a sandwich and something to drink.
She brought the girl a jacket to wear and had my father come to talk
to them to ask some questions so they can figure out if they were
runaways.

MIEKA: Wow. So what happened?

LOUISE: While my father was asking them questions, Grandma went to call
the law and said, "Come here, but don't use the sirens. Just come real
easy. He's talking to them and they're not going to run away nowhere.
They're just cold and tired." So she went back to them with a jacket
and said, "You should really go home." They said, "No, we don't want
to go home." Grandma said, "You know, the farther you get from
home the more dangerous it will be. You're lucky you found us. We
could have been bad people and do all kinds of bad things to you.
It's not safe. The farther away you get the more dangerous it gets."
Finally the little boy broke down and said, "OK, we'll go home." Then
Grandma went out and told the law that they can come. They drove
up and took the kids and brought them home.

MIEKA: I wonder why they were running away.

LOUISE: They were running away from home.

MIEKA: There might have been a good reason.

LOUISE: Yeah, they were being abused at home so they didn't want to go
there. But they said there was help for them.

While Louise "orients" the narrative by telling me that it happened "one time" (i.e., in the past), it seems unimportant to her to offer any more specific temporal orientation. Such a detail is insignificant to the point of history telling. Her use of the present participle as she begins the narrative ("hobos running around") suggests that though the event (obviously) happened in the past, its past-ness is not significant. Rather the story's significance lies in what the event says about the people involved. The story about the children on the railroad track was one with which most of Union's descendant residents were familiar—children do not show up on the Union's railroad tracks very frequently—and so, from Louise's perspective, the event did not require any temporal introductions. Instead, there is an opportunity in this rendition of the story to demonstrate the strength and character of the community. Coming together, they are able to successfully avert a potentially bad outcome (vulnerable children encountering bad people) and do so in a caring, nurturing way.

Moreover, this is also a story about how the community acts within— and even has influence on—"the law." Like Mr. Anderson's sit-in narrative, Louise also points out that the characters in her story are siding with "the law." This theme came up with some frequency in non-historical conversations with descendant residents as well. "The law"—denoting both the rules (prescribed behavior) and the organizations responsible for enforcing them (the police)—is used in conversation as a yardstick for assessing and managing people's behavior: a neighbor is said to deserve the ticket she got for letting her dog run loose because "she knows the law"; a mother, angered by her son's illicit activities, will threaten to "call the law" unless he stops. Descendant residents certainly have a real sense that laws are often unnecessarily overbearing and frequently enforced more harshly on African Americans than on white Americans. Despite (and perhaps because of) this fact, narrating residents' ability to work within the law—and even have the law work for them—serves as a powerful index both for their morality and their ability to successfully navigate an unjust legal system.

Fragmented History-Telling ("Turn Your
Head around, Boy!"/Jim Gaines)

Because the social exchanges among Union's descendant residents are embedded within dynamic, ongoing social interactions, any one rendition of an event from the past is not intended to be an exhaustive account of the events or experiences being recounted, nor is any single telling designed to stand alone as a disconnected, independent history. Fragments of histories can be invoked mid-conversation, acting merely as a component of a broader exchange, not as "complete" history. In this case, narrators might shift topics from past to present, seamlessly weaving together disparate temporalities without warning or qualification.

Spending time especially with Union's older descendant residents (in their seventies or older), I learned that an event could be invoked by simply mentioning one or two anchoring expressions. The same narrative might have different starting points on different occasions, and while an event or experience might sometimes be recounted in full (especially for outside researchers), more commonly only one element is invoked and linked to an otherwise unrelated conversation. As someone who was only partially proficient in residents' narrative repertoires, I usually managed to keep up with the general gist of a story, but not glean the multiple references made in the narratives—references that a "true" insider would be able to understand.

Among the Saramaka of Suriname, according to anthropologist and historian Richard Price, the sharing of historical knowledge is "deliberately incomplete." The Saramaka tell only fragments of stories, Price writes, and "will leave out most of what the teller knows about the incident in question" (2002:10). Further, Price notes that "such fragments make clear . . . why 'learning' a historical 'story' may take a full lifetime in this society" (2002:130).

Like the Saramaka, Union's residents too engage in a sort of "fragmented history-telling." Away from the tape recorders, only fragments of an event are offered at any one time, similarly "leav[ing] out most of

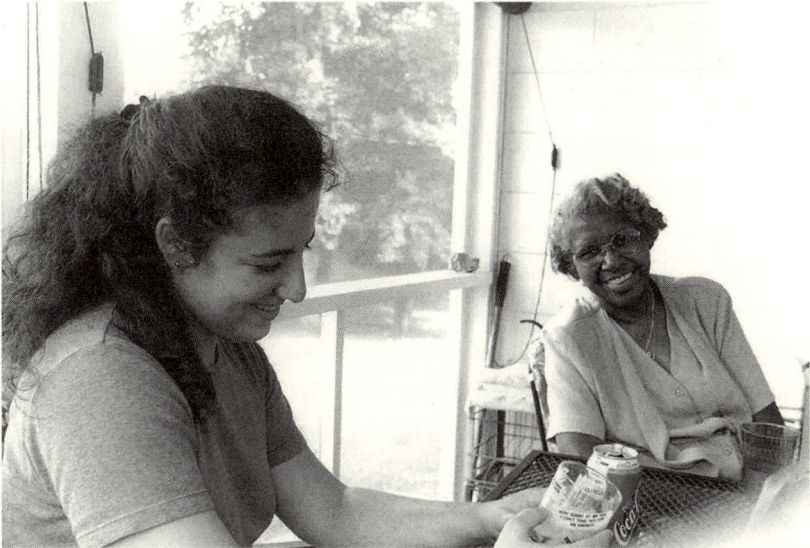

Julia Peters and Mieka Polanco, sitting on the porch at Ms. Peters's home. Photo by John Edwin Mason.

what the teller knows about the incident in question." In so doing, the listener is able to build a thick relationship to the historical event being described. The time lapse between hearing one fragment and another, the thoughts that complete the gaps in one's knowledge, even hearing different fragments from different narrators, all feed into a complex relationship to history and the past that could rival any Geertzian wink. Moreover, because narratives are not fixed, histories continue to have a dynamic social life. The fragments that I heard of any given story are different from the fragments another resident might have heard. Between us we form another layer of an already thick historical narrative.

On a quiet April afternoon, Mr. Gaines and I enjoyed lunch together while he amused himself by teaching me "old people expressions." My field notes are filled with descriptions of afternoons like this, sitting in the enclosed porch of his home, eating lunch from our favorite restaurant in town, Mr. Gaines chuckling as he gets me to repeat "old people expressions" or to speak "shop talk" (the very colorful and often less than flattering language common in black barbershops—including the one where Mr. Gaines worked for 35 years: "Look at old brick face. That boy so skinny, look like he whistling!").

"She's a buster" and "grounded" were the expressions du jour to which Mr. Gaines was introducing me. He invoked his grandmother's terms to describe an especially rotund neighbor. His eyes twinkled as he peered over to see if I was catching on. "It means she's big in here," he pointed at his stomach, choking up a laugh. Not answering, I laughed and shot a disapproving look his way. I wasn't going to talk trash about the neighbor. "She is a buster!" he repeated innocently. "You ever seen such fat knees on her?" Mr. Gaines was drawing on the sometimes pitiless manner his grandmother used to describe the people around her—a habit he had obviously and willingly inherited. Recalling the term must have reminded Mr. Gaines of his own experiences as the butt of "Mama's" harshness:

> MR. GAINES: She got some knees, ain't it? (pauses, as he awaits my
> response) You ain't gonna say nothing. (laughs)
> MIEKA: I've seen her knees.
> MR. GAINES: Honey, you ain't gonna . . . you won't comment on it.
> MIEKA: (laughing) No comment.
> [. . .]
> MR. GAINES: She grounded, yeah. That means shut up.
> MIEKA: Oh . . .
> MR. GAINES: My mama—my grandma used to scare me to death. Honey,
> I was a little boy and my grandmother would take me up to [the
> church in a neighboring community].
> MIEKA: Yeah.
> MR. GAINES: Church is still there.
> MIEKA: Yeah.
> MR. GAINES: Mama sat me on the front of the buggy. I was on the front—
> be sitting by her, too. I used to ride looking back. (imitates grand-
> mother) "Turn your head back here, boy!" (laughs) Couldn't even
> look at the back of the church! Old people were rough, honey.

MIEKA: Mm . . .

MR. GAINES: (imitates grandmother again) "Turn your head round. What you looking at?!" I said, "Nothing, Mama." She talking about the preacher up there and the man preaching. Old man Dabney Tanner was the preacher.

MIEKA: Old man what?

MR. GAINES: Dabney Tanner. He was the pastor. He was preaching his head off. (pause) Mama said, "Lord, Jeems, Look at old Dabney." Mama said he act like a gutted bull.

MIEKA: Mmm. Dabney Tanner . . .

MR. GAINES: (laughs) The way she talked about men . . . I tell you. My grandmother was something, she was.

MIEKA: Piece of work.

MR. GAINES: She was something. She said, "look like a gutted bull."

This narrative draws on a childhood memory—Grandma taking young James to visit a nearby church, and being "rough" as she demanded that he not look back. But why should he not look back during the ride? Since I had already heard fractions of this story previously, I knew that "old people" (of Mr. Gaines's grandmother's generation) used to say that the stretch of road between Union and the neighboring community (where Rev. Tanner's church was located) was haunted by a ghost. There is no need for him to clarify this detail, since he knew that I already knew it. Instead of focusing on details that are not important to this particular narration of the event (the ghost on the road to the church), Mr. Gaines emphasizes in this telling how his grandmother used to be "rough."

Mr. Gaines abbreviates superfluous details (glossed by using key anchoring terms) and stresses instead elements that are relevant for the point he is making. "Don't look back" indexes the haunted stretch of road, but puts the emphasis on Grandma's ability to "scare me to death." In quoting the grandmother calling her grandson "Jeems" (instead of "James"), Mr. Gaines alludes to the term of endearment used by his grandmother. When telling histories about his grandmother—and especially when they included him being reprimanded—Mr. Gaines would simply quote his matron, upset, calling out, "Come here, Jeems!"

In fact, "Jeems" serves a double function during this narration. First, it allows his interlocutors (me, in this case) to distinguish the speaker as Mr. Gaines's grandmother (whom he referred to as "Mama") as opposed to his wife (whom he also called "Mama") or even his biological mother (of whom he spoke less frequently, but sometimes also called "Mama"). His grandmother was the only one who called him "Jeems," and conjuring the special name allowed Mr. Gaines to index the tough-love upbringing that his grandmother provided—an upbringing of which Mr. Gaines was proud and whose decline he (and many of Union's older residents) lamented: Mama was "rough" and "scared me to death," but she also loved him, and had a special nickname for him.[4] The strict upbringing described by many of Union's descendant residents is frequently referred to by residents as a less than glamorous, but effective way to raise children. The narrative Mr. Gaines shares, then, is told in part to offer a lesson about the "proper" way children should be raised, compared to what he sees young parents do today.

Although I had access to some of the layers of reference offered in this short history, there were still other layers closed off to me, having met Mr. Gaines for the first time when he was 87 years old. For example, I did not have a context for why the pastor was "preaching his head off" (was he feeling the Spirit? possessed? an apparition?) or why his actions were likened to "a gutted bull" (how does a gutted bull act? Or was this a synonym for being "shut up," a "buster"—that is, fat?). At any rate, in this instance, the main gist of the narrative was to teach me "old people expressions" and through them a small window into the kind of world in which Mr. Gaines was raised.

The seamless transitions in Mr. Gaines's history from describing the neighbor as a "buster" and "grounded" to recounting how the grandmother forbade him from looking back on the road to describing the pastor's animated behavior, are reminders that each part of the conversation was not intended as a stand-alone, self-contained story. It is an exchange, an ongoing creation of social relationships through the invocation of stories about the past. As a researcher, I might be tempted to locate Mr. Gaines's early experiences within various social, political, and economic trajectories (Jim Crow, Depression era, or Union's then decidedly rural character, for example), but it is important to be aware that Mr. Gaines does not himself offer such a context.

The format of Mr. Gaines's history suggests that what I, the interlocutor, should focus on is not chronological trajectories but, among other things, a lesson about generational differences ("old people were rough, honey"), a lesson that both legitimizes and mitigates Mr. Gaines's own "rough" behavior to other (younger) people. As an "old person" himself now, history legitimizes Mr. Gaines's own unapologetic description of his rotund neighbor, and simultaneously mitigates it by demonstrating that, compared to his own "old people," he is really not so rough at all.

Conclusion

In recounting histories in casual contexts, Union residents produce narratives that are reflective of a complex experiential relationship to the past. Learning about the past is not considered a topic worth discussing in and of itself, but only worthwhile if it can elucidate some aspect of the present. Repetition allows descendant residents to co-produce "thick" insights into the past, producing an intimacy among insiders who can pick up on the embedded references, and a shared sense of identity and belonging to a community (which includes those "in the know"). The rendition of the sit-in experience that Mr. Anderson narrates is a lesson in maintaining an unwavering moral position despite an unjust legal system and an ambiguous moral situation. Ms. Celie's and Mr. Gaines's narratives about their respective disciplinarian grandmothers are in part commentaries on contemporary parenting skills as well as explanations of their own beliefs about child-rearing practices. Descendant residents tell histories not to build a chronological portrait of the past, but to enhance their own and their audiences' understandings of the present.

Telling history serves the multilayered purposes of weaving social networks, revealing new dimensions of a particular event (learning from the past), sharing an evolving perspective on life through the reexamination of past experiences, deepening social relations between narrator and interlocutor, and expanding an understanding of the present. While the histories that descendant residents offer during formal settings are descriptive and relatively flat, histories related in informal settings are rich and more dynamic, focusing less on facts and more on experiences. In informal settings, histories are repeated, fractured, described from varying angles and conjured in shifting contexts, yielding a three-dimensional "thick" relationship to the experiences and events being described.

In contrast with descendant residents or history brokers, Union's third group of residents—delegitimized historians—produce histories that reflect their own unique relationship to Union, to its meaning as an historical landscape, and to the very concept of community, as the following chapter unfolds.

4

"Not to Scale"

Cartographic Productions of Community

Each one of us, then, should speak of his roads, his crossroads, his roadside benches; each one of us should make a
surveyor's map of his lost fields and meadows. . . . Thus we
cover the universe with drawings we have lived. These drawings need not be exact. They need only to be tonalized on the
mode of our inner space.
Gaston Bachelard, *The Poetics of Space* (1994)

For map makers, their patrons, and their readers, the under-
class did not exist and had no geography, still less was it composed of individuals. . . . The peasantry, the landless labourers,
or the urban poor had no place in the social hierarchy and,
equally, as a cartographically disenfranchised group, they had
no right to representation on the map.
J. B. Harley, *Silences and Secrecy* (1988)

In late autumn 2001, I unexpectedly received in the mail a hand-drawn
map of Union. The map, a photocopy of the original, was reproduced
onto two large sheets of paper that were carefully taped together. The
cartographer was Ernest Greene. The sender was his cousin Peter Greene.
Both were raised in Union, but had moved away as young men. "Here
is a map that may be of interest to you," Peter introduced the piece in an
attached note. "It was prepared by my cousin, Ernest C. Greene, who is
88 years old, is well, rather alert, and loves to talk about history." At the

most densely depicted section on the paper, the word "Union," framed
by a thin black line, identified the geographical subject of the map. At
the lower right corner the cartographer had captioned his creation with
the words "NOT TO SCALE." Studying the map I tried to orient myself
within the space, but besides the railroad tracks traversing diagonally
across the page I did not recognize any feature in the landscape. It was
like looking at a map of a place I had never been to.

Given the focus of this book—an ethnography of the concept "community" in an officially recognized historically black community—the
map might seem like an unlikely subject to take up a chapter-length
discussion. The cartographer, Ernest Greene, is raced "white," was born
in a nearby county in 1913, moved to Union with his parents when he
was five years old, and lived there only until he married at the age of 21 in
1934. He is one of the few people I identify as "delegitimized historians"
with whom I sustained a long-term relationship—mostly thanks to his
persistence. Compared to the other residents with whom I interacted
during my research, Mr. Greene probably lived in Union the least amount
of time—and the longest time ago.

But it is precisely this spatial and temporal distance from Union
that made Mr. Greene's map so analytically poignant. For while he may
have spent the least time physically living in Union, his relationship
to the place and especially to its official history divulges none of that
distance, and appears seamlessly to connect past and present, "here"
and "there," Mr. Greene and Union. This chapter focuses on productions and expressions of community by residents I am calling "delegitimized historians." A detailed analysis of the map drafted by Mr. Greene
offers insights into the ways history, space, and race collectively form a
sense of community that is unique to this particular group of people.
While they are invested in history telling as a nationalist project, they
simultaneously also tend to read themselves as invisible in official historical narratives. Greene's map—a visual representation of Union as
he remembered it from his youth—allows us to explore some of this
spatio-temporal complexity.

Ernest Greene's hand-drawn map of Union. Drafted by Ernest Greene, 1998.

When Mr. Greene's map arrived in my mailbox I had been working in Union for a little over a year, and though there was still much for me to learn about it, I was already quite familiar with the physicality of this tiny locale: the two main roads traversing it, Mt. Zion Baptist Church, the now-abandoned general merchandise store, the old and new houses lining Union Road, the narrow dirt roads linking the houses to one another. . . . I remember searching on the map for a representation of the church (which had been built in 1888), thinking that once I pinpointed it in relation to the railroad tracks I could triangulate my way through the rest of the landscape. But the church was nowhere to be found. I tried to identify some roads that I knew existed prior to 1934 (the date the map is said to represent), but they were not labeled and I was unable even to identify Union Road, the biggest and most easily recognizable road in Union. I ran through the family names that were carefully recorded beside each house hoping to come across one that I recognized, but there were none that I knew. Instead, I found myself rotating the sheet at every possible angle, trying to gain some footing in the landscape.

In the midst of my mounting frustration, I suddenly decoded the legend to Greene's map. Mt. Zion Church was not on Greene's map because Mt. Tabor, the white Baptist church down the road, was. None of the names by the houses were familiar to me because they represented long-time white residents, who were rarely part of the social circles I was familiar with: descendant residents or history brokers. Indeed, this was a map of a place I had never been to.

Mr. Greene, who left Union many years before it was conferred the status of a Historic District, drew a map of Union that represents the place he remembered from his own youth (a subsequent copy of the map, which I received directly from Ernest Greene later in my fieldwork, includes his added note: "Drawn by Ernest Carlton Greene, as remembered—1918–1934"). Even though the church and some of the roads and homes I knew were in existence before 1934, the map depicted a lily-white community with no signs of any African American presence whatsoever. The homes of descendant residents among whom I conducted most of my fieldwork, the roads leading to their homes, and even Mt. Zion Baptist Church—which the NRHP identifies as Union's "visual landmark"—were all completely absent.

On the other hand, more recent features in the landscape that were built after 1934 (including a nearby multilane highway and small airport) were included in the map, even though the map is supposed to depict Union at an earlier time. This was the most direct visual representation I could imagine, whether conscious or not, of almost complete racial erasure. Even though residents raced both "black" and "white" all physically inhabited the same locale and their homes were interspersed among each other, the map suggests that this was a space in which racial groups were so absolutely separate that they literally inhabited different planes of existence. Was each group really entirely blind to the other? Was it simply Mr. Greene's privileged position as a white man that allowed him to systematically skip over the homes of his black neighbors and actively not-see (and not-remember) them? "Not to scale" came to take on a new meaning as I continued studying this map, and "scale" eventually became a central analytical tool for making sense of what had been depicted in this geographical portrayal of Union.

This chapter is something of a "topoanalysis" (Bachelard 1994) of Greene's map. It is a study of the map as a culturally meaningful activity—its making, its representations of space and history, its placement within given socio-political contexts, and ultimately, its reflection on how community is produced and experienced.

The virtually complete absence of African American spaces in Greene's map could be seen as an easily legible statement about race relations in Union between 1918 and 1934. It might be read as a straightforward manifestation of racially motivated disempowerment, silencing, and erasure. Such a reading would be mostly accurate, but a deeper reading allows us to use the map as an entryway into a more revealing, more detailed look at the spaces of memory, and especially of home, for a white resident whose "home" has been officially recognized as a historically black community. Although the map claims to reflect Union between 1918 and 1934 (the years Mr. Greene resided in Union), it was not drafted until 1998 and reflects not only more than six decades of Union's transformation into a place of nostalgia for Mr. Greene, but also late-20th-century sensibilities and socio-political dynamics.

Considering the map as a social text, this chapter is organized into two sections: I begin with an analysis of the process of creating the map. This section focuses on its particular contents, particularly Ernest Greene's choices of what to include and what not to include in his geography of Union. Next I look at the map as an object, a thing-in-the-world that has social, symbolic meaning beyond its particular contents. In this second section I consider the map's social life outside the intentions and control of its cartographer, focusing particularly on the map as a material, written record about the past, and considering the significance of the existence of multiple copies of the map.

Creating a Map I: Choosing What to Include

The map charted by Ernest Greene is a guide—but unlike most maps, the contours on Greene's map are not meant to usher viewers to move their bodies across a physical landscape. Instead, and perhaps more like the experience of viewing a landscape painting than a map (Casey 2002), viewers of his map are asked to move their imagined bodies through imagined space—and, indeed, imagined time—back to Mr. Greene's youth, tracing hand-drawn roads that do not correspond to physical landscape, but to a memory-scape, where experiences are embodied at a different "scale." Viewers are invited to reflect rather than move, to notice nuances, make the place familiar, remember it along with the remembering cartographer, and experience Union as a young Ernest Greene once had.

Having drafted the map many decades after he had experienced the place, however, Mr. Greene's invitation to experience Union is not precisely "as a young Ernest Greene once had." Rather, viewing the map is more of a reflection of his present memories of the place, rather than what it had been in his youth. Not so much a map of place, this is a map of a memory of a long-ago place. The map offers not only a 70-year perspective on what Union used to mean to Mr. Greene while he was growing up, but also a perspective on his relationship to the place at the time he charted it. Although by 2002 he hadn't lived in Union for several decades, his home was only about 20 miles away and, having worked in construction projects throughout Piedmont County most of his life, he has canvassed the region extensively and maintained an ongoing relationship with others who continued to live in Union and with Calvary Church where he used to worship as a child.

At the time he drafted the map, Ernest Greene, then 85, and his cousin Peter, 68, had been involved for more than ten years in researching their family roots, tracing records of their ancestors back as early as they could. Peter, who was a chemist before he retired, left his scientific pursuits and developed a new interest in genealogical research. Ernest, on the other hand, had already been interested in historical and genealogical research for many years. His career in construction spanned nearly six decades and certainly filled up a good portion of his days, but the piles of books about Thomas Jefferson, the Second World War, and especially the Civil War that line his small living room, and the innumerable stacks of family papers adorning every corner of the house, disclose that learning and thinking about history are not, for Mr. Greene, novel pursuits.

The elements that Mr. Greene remembered and chose to depict on his map of Union reflect this long-standing relationship with history making and historical records. The map demonstrates a consciousness of the role that documents play in producing formal histories, and is simultaneously a historical resource (in that it provides "facts" that can be drawn upon to produce histories) and a historical narrative (in that it tells a story about Union's past).[1] As such, the map is revealing both of the social world in which Ernest Greene lived as a child, and of the contemporary social context within which it was drawn. "Both in the selectivity of their content and in their signs and styles of representation," writes social geographer J. B. Harley, "maps are a way of conceiving, articulating, and structuring the human world which is biased towards, promoted by, and exerts influence upon particular sets of social relations" (2001:53).

Like written histories, maps are the product of a selection process undertaken by the mapmaker. As narratives about space, even maps that claim to be complete are only images "within which (and between which) very much more is left out than is put in" (Lévi-Strauss 1966:257). Faced with a dilemma parallel to that of the historian's—the impossibility of representing in the map everything that physically exists on the ground—cartographers must choose what of the landscape they wish to include and what can be omitted in order to make a legible statement about the terrain. As a result, the selection of contents and styles of representation in the map reflect some of the social relations that structure the cartographer's world. The interplay between inclusion and omission, presence and absence in Greene's map is revealing about his conceptualization of Union as a community, and the very "scales" of the map—the spatial and temporal axes upon which it hinges—are rich with social significance.

The map Mr. Greene drew is said to represent Union during his youth, but it was drafted in 1998, shortly before a biannual Greene family reunion, when he was in his mid-eighties, and during the same year that Union received its official recognition as a historically black community. The convergence of these three temporal elements (the reunion, Greene's age, and official recognition) contribute much to what was remembered and chosen to be depicted in the map.

Mapping Social Relations

As one of the oldest members of the Greene family, Ernest Greene frequently plays a key role in organizing family reunions. Preparing for the 1998 event, which was scheduled to be held at Calvary Church, his old home-church on Union Road, he was inspired to sketch a map that outlined the spatial perimeters of his community during his youth. It was not prepared specifically for the reunion (and in fact, he did not bring it to the 1998 event—though it has been on display in subsequent reunions), though undoubtedly preparations for the event conjured memories and thoughts about what younger generations might want (and need) to remember about the family and about Union.

The map includes representations of places that Ernest Greene would have been intimately and immediately familiar with—his home, the church where his family had worshipped, the school he attended, his grandfather's store, the family cemetery. And it also includes places with which he would have been less familiar—places some distance from his home, belonging to a slightly more extended circle of acquaintances, or institutions (like Mt. Tabor Church) of which he was not a part. In fact, most of the terrain depicted on Greene's map lies outside the area that he most closely associates with "home," and even outside the area that he identifies as "Union proper." Mr. Greene drew a circle around the area on the map he identifies as Union proper, captioned it with the word "Union," and included more detail in it than in any other part of the map. The outlying areas, on the other hand, are not given names or borders and gradually fade from dense to sparse as their distance from Union increases.

Why did Mr. Greene decide to draft a map, and why did he choose the projection and parameters that he did? During a phone conversation, he told me that he drew the map for his cousin Peter, who was preparing a genealogy of their family. By creating a map—a statement about place—which could then be drawn on to prepare a narrative about the Greene family history, Ernest Greene could make a statement about the existence of a strong relationship between his kinfolk and the terrain depicted in the map.

Growing up in Union, Ernest Greene was surrounded by a large and close-knit family. Many of his relatives also lived in and around Union, most in families with eight or more children, making for a social world comprised prominently by members of his own family. In the time we spent together, Mr. Greene would often recall this experience, describing a sense of never being alone, always being surrounded by relatives. By contrast, the younger generation who now attend family reunions are scattered around the country and travel to Virginia only long enough to attend the reunions.

The intimate experience of family that Mr. Greene would recount from his youth is today all but gone, replaced by far-away relatives who stay in touch by telephone or email and visit only occasionally. Mr. Greene himself spends a fair amount of time with his daughter, with whom he lives, but only infrequently with other family members. More than once he lamented that he and Peter were "the last ones left. . . . The last generation." In the face of what he perceives as an endangered family line, land is the one constant remnant of his youth that continues to exist unconditionally despite a shifting social world.

Capturing this terrain on a map and offering it to his extended family, to this young, scattered-about generation, Union becomes a proxy for the experience of community that Mr. Greene once had—and for the experience that the new generation could potentially recreate. Drawing a map that includes not only those places that he frequented most but a broad regional depiction of the area was a way for him to claim the entire landscape as a home-place. As a feature in family reunions, the map becomes an ancestral anchor for those who have drifted away, charting in some sense a road map towards a once-again close-knit and family-oriented community.

Leaving a Legacy

Ernest Greene's age at the time he drafted the map is also significant for understanding its meaning to the cartographer. In his mid-eighties when he drew the map, he found himself spending a lot of time reflecting on his life experiences and the legacy he will leave behind. Most of the people in his circle of friends are younger, and he is acutely aware that few share his memories of places and events and that, without a permanent record, his own memories too will disappear with his passing. During our meetings, Mr. Greene would regularly point out to me that he has "personal memories" of topics we read about in history books, or he would try to express something of the proximity he feels to certain "historic moments." As he explained one afternoon:

> MR. GREENE: General Custer turned around and went over the bridge
> and set the mill afire with all the grain in it. And burned it. And my
> grandmother witnessed that. And she was still living when I was
> born. So that hooks me right back to the Civil War!
> MIEKA: Yeah, I guess it does.
> MR. GREENE: I was born 40 years after, and it's been 56 . . . 57 years since
> World War Two was over.
> MIEKA: Right . . .
> MR. GREENE: So the Civil War was just as fresh in my grandparents mind
> as World War Two is now to us!

But since "personal memories" alone do not guarantee a continued legacy after death, Mr. Greene did his best to ensure that the stories he tells of his own lifetime of experiences will be preserved even after he himself is gone. In the years I knew him, he was incredibly prolific, producing material recordings (written, drawn, audio- and videotaped) that complemented the histories he would tell me about himself and his family.

Within two or three weeks of our first meeting, my "Ernest Greene" folder was already bulging with documents and notes (including multiple copies of the map) that he had prepared and wanted to share with me. I would explain that my project was not a recording of Union's history, but rather an analysis of the meaning of history to various residents, but he continued to greet me with piles of documents, videotapes, or maps that he "thought [I] may be interested in," and he inquired regularly about how my writing was coming along. Given the amount of documents Mr. Greene had accumulated, I would sometimes jokingly suggest that he should be writing a dissertation (and earning a Ph.D.) instead of me. I am not entirely sure he disagreed.

In addition to the documents Mr. Greene had prepared himself, many documents he handed to me were published materials—but even these were filled with his annotations—explanations of how he fit into the larger narrative. A photograph of a house in a history book about Piedmont County, for example, includes his note: "Ernest C. Greene drew plans and built the wing attaching the kitchen on the yard to the main log home. Added a large kitchen to the back of this and added a bath on the second floor. Put in a forced hot air system for all in 1960. ECG."

Knowing that well-kept documents can potentially have long "shelf lives," inserting his own narratives into those documents were a way for Mr. Greene to assert his "native-ness" to the land, and ensure that his own legacy would continue along with the historical documents. Furthermore, since he knows that material records (in contrast with those orally transmitted, for example) frequently serve as primary sources in the writing of histories, a carefully drafted and judiciously preserved map can serve as one effective way to vie for "a place in history"[2] even after death.

A Place in History

In some sense, Ernest Greene is uniquely positioned to produce histories—that is, written records about the past—of Union. Not only does he
remember Union in the 1920s and 1930s, he also understands the underpinnings of mainstream history production. Having spent years reading and studying formal histories, learning through them about people,
places and events that are said to be significant, he has a sense of what
formal histories should look like, how they should be written, what type
of information needs to be included, and what should be left out. In 2002
he handed me a historical essay that he was in the process of writing.
Entitled "Some Recollections of the Village of [Union, Piedmont Co.],
Va." The essay begins, "In 1920, when I was seven years old, my father,
the Rev. Walter H. Greene, bought out the other heirs to his parents'
homeplace. The farm was located on [Union Road], right behind the old
original [Calvary Christian Church] building, which still stands today."

The format of this 14-page history was modeled after the history books
in Mr. Greene's collection: it is inundated with the full and proper names
of people and places, recording the year or approximate range of years
when events took place, and covering such topics as social structure
("the railroad station had two waiting rooms, one for white passengers,
and one for colored folks"), economy ("in 1920, there were four general
stores"), and major events ("the school burned down on March 8, 1934,
three years after I graduated"). But throughout, as in the first sentence
and despite the essay's title, he ensures that his version of Union's history
is inseparable from his own personal (and family) history—so much so
that a reader could almost assume that Union sprang to life when the
Greene family moved to the area, and dissipated after Ernest Greene
moved away.

Similarly in the map, Mr. Greene is mindful to locate this visual history within a specific historical period and place, and infuses the landscape with his own relationship to it. Some elements of this are relatively
overt, like a dotted line connecting his home to the schoolhouse, labeled

"Path to school. About 2 miles." Others, like the map's shifting spatial scale, are less obvious: areas that were part of his immediate world are carefully depicted and more detailed than other parts of the map. As a result they are represented on a relatively large scale, taking up a disproportionate amount of space on the map. Accordingly, parts of the landscape with which he was less familiar end up being represented on a much smaller scale, taking up relatively less space on the page than their physical counterparts on the ground, and including much less detail.

Because Mr. Greene was more familiar with the structures in his immediate surroundings, these are not only slightly larger than other structures, but also more detailed. His grandfather's store, for example, is depicted with a fairly precise rendition of the building's layout and a bird's-eye perspective of the roof. It is labeled "J.C. Greene Store." Another more distant store, on the other hand, is drawn simply as a square and is indistinguishable from the surrounding houses, except that the words "Turner Store" are noted beside it.

While Mr. Greene may have paid closer attention to the places with which he would have been most familiar (home, church, school, etc.), there are no deliberate markings to denote that the cartographer had any special relationship to them. So, for example, the store is identified with the owner's family name and first two initials—"J.C. Greene Store"— but it does not read "Ernest Greene's grandfather's store." Although the words on the map do not immediately reveal the cartographer's greater physio-emotional proximity to one area over another, the map's spatial scale helps tell this history without the need for overt (and therefore indiscreet) statements about it.

As mentioned above, the copy of the map that Mr. Greene handed me included a caption he added: "Drawn by Ernest C. Greene, as remembered 1918–1934." Thinking of me as a sort of historian, he entrusted me with a copy of the map precisely because he assumed he could live on through the map both as history in itself and as a historical object. The map forms a visual history of Union, one that is thoroughly infused with his personal memories (and therefore legacy). As a historical resource, the caption to Greene's map ensures that researchers like me—affiliated with a university and whose writing is more likely to have a broad audience through publication—are very clear about who authored the map, and whose world it is said to represent. Indeed, that this chapter focuses on Mr. Greene's map proves that he was not entirely incorrect in assuming that I would draw on his work as a rich source of knowledge (even if not quite in the way he imagined). As an academic, it would be appropriate to credit him with the creation of the map. It is somewhat regretful—for me, but especially from Mr. Greene's perspective—that in my commitment to keep the real names of Union's residents private, his name and legacy are obscured by a pseudonym.

White Spaces on the Map

With only one exception—Mill River snaking around three sides of the page's borders—the map exclusively depicts features that are human made. Located in rural Virginia, Union is fairly lush, containing wooded areas and much vegetation, as well as several brooks and ponds. But Mr. Greene chose to exclude these features from the landscape and focus singularly on human-made features. There are no signs denoting "natural" features such as hills (or elevation markings), bodies of water, or vegetation.[3] Even gardens, which straddle an already problematic distinction between "natural" and "human made," are not represented in Greene's map. Instead, the topography of the map focuses on houses, roads, property lines, and other manmade landmarks. As a historical narrative, then, this map is centered specifically on Union's terrain of social interaction.

Around Union proper, the omission of "natural" spaces is barely noticeable because the enlarged houses fill up most of what would otherwise be blank spots on the map. But even in the outlying areas where less detail is provided, very few spaces are unaccounted for. Instead of leaving blank those areas where woods or ponds exist, potentially leading the viewer to question what is missing, Mr. Greene fills in the landscape with lines—presumably approximating property lines—that partition the paper into contiguous, adjoining sections. Each section sits flush against the property beside it and has a family name written across the enclosed area. The result is a map in which there are almost no unaccounted-for spaces. The partitions ensure that even the "white spaces" on the map—areas that do not have anything drawn on them—are accounted for and given social meaning by turning them into "white space"—areas that are associated with one of the white families living in Union.

A Perforated-Line Landscape

Crisscrossing these maps are the main arteries of traffic, as Mr. Greene recalled their approximate layout during his youth. They include some roads that continue to exist, but also some that are no longer in use, or that have become tertiary dirt roads today serving predominantly as driveways to private homes. On the other hand, there are also two roads on the map that did not come into existence until after the period said to be depicted on the map: one that was not built until the 1950s, and the other built in the 1930s, but represented in the map as the expanded multilane highway it now is.

Although the map is chronologically focused on the years Mr. Greene lived in Union, its temporal scale is skewed slightly—and consciously—to include features from more recent times. Both of the temporally infringing roads (representing contemporary rather than historical arteries) were gingerly added, depicted only by perforated lines cutting across the historical landscape. Since one road is a well-traveled route, and the other leads to a commonly recognized regional airport, both would likely be familiar features to contemporary viewers. Depicting them on the map, Mr. Greene offers the two roads as spatial anchors to viewers who are familiar with the region's current terrain. In recognizing the perforated-line roads and noticing the historical landscape they traverse, such viewers can then "connect the dots," superimposing the solid-lined historical landscape of the map atop an implied perforated-line, present-day landscape of their own experiences. In this way, the roads act as a sort of portal into the imagined history-time of the map.

Like the experience of looking at an old photograph of a place one currently knows, viewers who recognize the contemporary perforated-line roads are invited to match up places they know with the places they see in the map and delight in the excitement of discovery: "Oh, so that is what this place used to look like!" Chances are that the delight experienced by such a viewer would not be hedged with a critical questioning of what was depicted on the map or, more importantly, what was not. And yet it is this very question that reminds us that the map is not an unmitigated facsimile of the historical terrain, but rather a history in itself: a visual representation of Mr. Greene's memory-scape of his youth.

Creating a Map II: Choosing What to Leave Out

The most overt and analytically curious omission in the map is, as indicated earlier, the lack of any reference whatsoever to the presence of African American residents in Union. My interactions with other (black and white) residents from the area, examinations of census records and postal route maps from the 1920s and 1930s, and even conversations with Mr. Greene himself all indicate that Union had been racially heterogeneous long before he and his family moved to the area, and that the homes of African American and white residents were interspersed among each other—even if the groups were socially segregated.

Despite this, even though Union's predominantly black church (Mt. Zion) and its white counterpart (Mt. Tabor) stood less than one mile apart on the same stretch of Union Road, Mr. Greene (who attended a third church farther down the road) depicts only Mt. Tabor on his map. Further, unlike the layout of more urban settlements in the area during the time depicted in the map, Union had not been physically segregated along racial lines:[4] the homes of the Gaineses, Farradays, and Marshalls—African American families living in Union at the time—were interspersed among those of the Wades, Turners, and Greenes—their white neighbors. Nonetheless, only the homes of the latter show up on Greene's map, while the former remain invisible.

Here again, we see "scale" being gently massaged into telling a particular history of the place. In the spaces where African Americans' homes would have been present, the homes of white families are depicted as slightly too large. Their scale is expanded ever so slightly so they take up too much space on the map relative to the physical structures they are said to represent. As in the omission of "natural" features in the landscape, here too potentially conspicuous gaps between the houses are made invisible, leaving neatly lined family homes abutting each other and a benign statement about the terrain of a close-knit (white) community.

Uncultivated Non-Spaces

The schematic format of the map, traceable to the slightly shaky hand of an elderly cartographer and the qualifying note "not to scale," incline viewers to be forgiving about any geometric miscalculations or omissions, and no cartographic breadcrumbs are left for the curious viewer wondering about more curious distortions. No map, after all, is a precise mimesis of the landscape it is said to represent, and hand-drawn maps (we tend to believe) are all the more prone to inaccuracy. As I described above, a close study of the map reveals that the houses, for example, are too large relative to the represented terrain, but their spatial distortion becomes simply a feature of imprecise, unscientific scaling. The too-small gaps left between too-large houses blend into the overall hand-drawn character of the map, rendering the gaps either entirely unnoticeable, or simply concealing uncultivated, unacculturated non-spaces. The names recorded beside each house take up even more blank space on the map, further aiding in the erasure of unaccounted-for areas—and at any rate building an expectation that some detail must be omitted to allow room for the recording of names.

There are no direct statements about racial politics in the map. A viewer unfamiliar with the landscape might not even notice the disproportionately sized houses or the shifting scaling and re-scaling of space. Rather, the houses depicted in Mr. Greene's map inconspicuously

meander along the various roads, their owners' names unassumingly presented beside each. No clue gives away the fact that over a dozen houses
were left out of this rendition of the landscape, nor that these belonged
specifically to Union's African American families. Instead, the statements
made in the map about racial politics are subtle, polite, genteel. One
might even wonder whether they are indiscernible to the cartographer
himself, or whether my analysis is making a to-do of something that is
not really there.

Ernest Greene was born to a white family in Virginia early in the
20th century and raised at a time when segregation and social, political, and economic discrimination against African Americans were not
only acceptable but legislated. Mr. Greene, who participated in (and benefited from) the segregated system as much as any of his white peers,
could afford to draft a lily-white map of Union as a privileged member
of society who (especially in the 1920s and 1930s) did not need to put
effort into including his less privileged black neighbors. The rendition
of Union depicted in the map can be read as simply a depiction of his
social universe as a young person: one in which African Americans and
white Americans interacted only when necessary, in power-imbalanced
situations, and were otherwise entirely separate from one another. But
such a reading would be incorrect. As happens everywhere, lived experiences are inevitably more "messy" than laws would have it, and social
segregation between Union's white and black residents was rarely airtight.

In his written memoirs, Mr. Greene notes that his own father, "a traveling evangelist," sometimes preached at Mt. Zion, the local black church.
As a construction worker, furthermore, Mr. Greene himself remembers
having labored alongside black co-workers throughout his career, even
during the height of legislated segregation. And, living in a rural, semi-
agricultural community,[5] Union residents came together at particular
moments across—and despite—racial lines, depending upon one another
during hog-killing time and fire emergencies.

Over the course of my fieldwork, many residents cited hog-killing
time (which required more pairs of hands than were usually available in

one household) and house fires (when as much help as could be summoned on short notice was essential) as sort of "communitas" moments
in which racial identity temporarily lost social significance. On these
occasions residents came together to help each other even if they otherwise had no contact, because these two very different kinds of events
represented concerns shared by most residents. If you didn't cooperate
when someone else was in need, I was told, you risked being abandoned
when you found yourself in need.

Cartographically Disenfranchised

Given these somewhat porous racial boundaries that Ernest Greene
traversed during his youth in Union, why then did he so meticulously
erase the social spaces of people whom he at least knew about, even if
he was not socially close to? After all, there are other households that
were relatively insignificant to Mr. Greene, but that he depicted nonetheless. As suggested above, one simple explanation is to assume that these
omissions are a reflection of gaps in his memory. Growing up in Union
during the 1920s and 1930s, this map could be a representation of racial
segregation: the houses that he left out belonged to people with whom
he came into contact only rarely. Conjuring the landscape after having
lived elsewhere for nearly 70 years, it is understandable that he might
overlook houses that played only a minor role in his life. But what of
Mt. Zion Church, where his father sometimes preached? What of the
fact that many of these landmarks do show up in his written memoirs,
recorded at a different time and for different purposes? And what of
the fact that the map was drafted in the same year that the Union Community Association was completing its final draft of an application for
historical recognition?

Even if Mr. Greene had forgotten most of Union's African American
residents, there clearly seems to be an active "de-recollection" of anything
African American in the map. He remembers elements of Union's black
social spaces in his written memoirs, but these are left out entirely in the

map. It is apparent that even though he remembers some of the African American families residing in Union during his youth, these families are not relevant to the particular history of Union that he recounts in his map.

In an interview conducted and videotaped in 1996 by one of Union's history brokers, Mr. Greene stood outside what had once been Union's train depot. A newcomer neighbor stopped by to find out the reason for the videotaping, and a conversation ensued between the two men (who were strangers to each other). As the tape rolls, Mr. Greene recalls some of his African American neighbors:

> MR. GREENE: And when I was brought up here on the farm, we had eight
>   slaves to work on our farm.
> NEIGHBOR: (slightly sarcastically) Is that right?
> MR. GREENE: (sincerely) Yes!
> NEIGHBOR: Back that far, huh?
> MR. GREENE: Yeah, they told me stories about back during the Civil War.

Given Mr. Greene's enthusiasm for Civil War history, it is all the more notable that even the "slaves" that he claims to remember in conversation are not present in the map. It is not the case, then, that he forgot there was a black community in Union during his youth, but rather that—like the 16th-century European mapmakers described by J. B. Harley—for Mr. Greene, this community "did not exist and had no geography, still less was it composed of individuals" (1988:68).

African American residents were, to Mr. Greene, not neighbors, but nameless "slaves" (an interesting term, marked also by the neighbor's response, since Mr. Greene was describing a period some 50 years after slavery was abolished). While his grandmother's memory of the Civil War links him with this period, his experiences with Union's black residents obviously did not have the same effect. As nothing more than slaves, black residents have "no place on the social hierarchy and, equally, as a cartographically disenfranchised group, they had no right to representation on the map" (Harley 1988:68). It was not forgetting, then, but an active leaving out that kept African American households off the Greene map.

"Home" as a Historically Black Community

The socio-temporal context within which Greene's map was drafted is also important for understanding the omission of African American spaces in it. Besides being the year of a Greene family reunion, 1998 was also when Union's history brokers were preparing to submit their completed application for official recognition of Union as a historically black community. This process had taken nearly two years to complete. I am not entirely sure when Mr. Greene first learned about the nomination or its approval by the National Register of Historic Places, but by 1998 he certainly already knew about it. During our very first phone conversation he asked me whether I had met Mr. Lawson. "He's the one who designated Union as a historic village," Mr. Greene explained. "He was supposed to interview me about the history of Union a long time ago, but we never did it. Maybe you can talk to him." I said I would.

To Ernest Greene, Union represents an emotionally charged memory-scape. It is a space bound up with his recollections of his early life and family. It is a community to which he felt a powerful sense of belonging. Though he was never so crass as to put it to me in these terms, official recognition of Union as a historically black community was undoubtedly a blow on at least three counts. First, by recognizing Union as an exclusively black space, his own claims to membership in the community were quickly delegitimized. There is no hint in the title "historically black community" that white residents lived in Union at all, let alone were integral to its social fabric. His own claims to the space—especially as a site of history—become marginal and mostly inaudible in the shadow of a hegemonic state-sanctioned narrative about Union's "official" monochromatic identity.

Second, in Union's official recognition as a historically black community, Mr. Greene not only loses a legitimated claim over the (history of

Civil War reenactors, Memorial Day ceremony, 2002, Riverton, Virginia. Photo by Mieka Brand Polanco.

the) space, but he loses it to people whom he does not necessarily consider worthy of history. As he would consistently remind me in our many hours of interviews, his family owned farmland, they were soldiers in the Civil War, and they "had slaves." In other words, they personified all the qualities required to be counted as "important" in ways that hegemonic mainstream histories consider relevant. Those African American families who were included in Union's official history, on the other hand, came from modest means, some themselves having been slaves (according to his memory, well into the 20th century!). They did not have the same access to power as Mr. Greene and his family, and they certainly did not measure up according to the traditional standards of "importance" of official histories.

In the piles of history books filling up Mr. Greene's house, African Americans play a minor role, at best. Black Americans—"slaves"—serve as background characters in narratives about the lives of "important" people such as President Thomas Jefferson or the explorers Lewis and

Clark. They show up in the margins of books about the Second World War, and take a back seat in tales about battles, skirmishes, strategic planning, and the deplorable living conditions of Confederate soldiers during the Civil War. Yet, it is precisely these apparently "unimportant" residents who receive national historic recognition, and to whom Mr. Greene must concede defeat in the question of who can legitimately stake a claim for Union and its official history.

Third, Union's recognition means that this now officially black space is identified as historic, a label with which Mr. Greene is closely familiar and deeply respectful. This final blow is, perhaps, the most stinging. Mr. Greene spent many hours and considerable amounts of ink seeking recognition (official or otherwise) for his own family history. As described earlier, historical and genealogical research have been favorite pastimes of his for many years, and after retirement he spent more time than ever conducting historical research and thinking about his own history and genealogy. The books that he and his cousin wrote are self-published and the two always make sure to provide copies of their works to local historical societies and libraries. He fills his personal collection of history books with annotations, recording for example that a certain author is "my personal friend" or describing connections between a place named in a history book and his own family history.

On the other hand, from Mr. Greene's perspective Union's black residents had invested almost no work in the nomination process (most was done, as described earlier, by history-broker residents and paid historians), yet they managed to attain national historic recognition. The courteous but relatively indifferent response of many of Union's descendant residents to the unsolicited "gift" of official recognition was perhaps proof to him that they were unworthy subjects of history. Black residents did not even seem to be impressed (as Mr. Greene might have been) with the title Historic District that Union now claims.

In the face of all this, drawing a map that portrays Union as an exclusively white space can be read as a defiant challenge to the hegemonic narrative and the very premise for historic recognition. In another time and context, we might have called this cartographic act a form of resistance: Mr. Greene, who associates himself with the Confederate army (for example through membership in the Sons of Confederate Veterans), with old-guard white Southerners—and therefore on the "wrong side of history"—charts a map that contradicts in its most basic terms the state-approved reading of the landscape. The map can be read as a deliberate assertion of an alternative vision of Union as a historic site to that produced by the history brokers. From Ernest Greene's perspective, history brokers (if for no other reason than their lack of ancestral roots in Union) had a tenuous relationship to Union's history—and yet it was they who oversaw the production of Union's official history.

Though others might not perceive him as such, in some ways Mr. Greene regards himself as a member of a marginalized group (mainstream society looks down upon and marginalizes Southern whites and their proud heritage). Another resident, one of those I identify as "delegitimized historians," once confided in me, "I think it's really great that you're doing a project that shows that the separation isn't as real as people say it is. Things weren't quite as bad as people would have you think." I had just finished describing my project to this resident, explaining that although Union is identified as a black community, I was aware that "there are people who aren't black who live there, too. I'm trying to put together a project that includes all of the residents." The resident expressed his deep support for what he perceived was a revised history, and named some neighbors he thought would be appropriate for me to speak to. All those he mentioned would be considered white, and none had been interviewed for the NRHP nomination. "You may want to talk to them," the man told me, "they have a lot of history." As best I could, I contacted each of the residents he listed, and interviewed all who were willing.

For his part, Mr. Greene nominated himself to fill in the gaps in Union's official history. His "act of resistance," then, was directed towards what delegitimized historian residents perceived as an act of silencing by hegemonic mainstream culture. It was a way to reclaim the interview that never happened, and insert himself into his rightful "place in history." Where his family had been rooted, official recognition placed their own version of "blank spaces," seeing only a monochromatic black geography. Whether or not the map should be considered an act of resistance (and any conclusive verdict is in any case less important than understanding the map's multiple layers of signification), it is apparent that for Mr. Greene drafting a counter-hegemonic visual history of Union was a way to assert a subversive voice in the state-produced history of the place.

The Social Life of Greene's Map

The map drawn by Ernest Greene was not intended for public use. It is a record that circulates primarily among family members and friends. Nor was it intended to be a comprehensive sketch of Union. Rather, it is a personal reflection by an elderly man of the social world of his youth and of his relationship to the place 70 years after he moved away. It is a landscape of memory and experiences, not of exacting scientific depiction. Indeed, to avert any misunderstanding or confusion, Mr. Greene clearly qualifies his cartographic creation with the words "not to scale."

But regardless of what Mr. Greene may have intended, as a map—a physical, cultural thing in the world—his creation holds meaning. Until now I have analyzed the map from the standpoint of its creator: the choices Mr. Greene made about what to include and what to omit, and the way scale is employed to tell a narrative about Union and its past. But a map, besides containing a visually communicated message by the cartographer, is itself an object that has meaning and value within the social structure regardless of (and sometimes despite) the intentions of its creator. Here I draw on Appadurai's (1988) discussion of things as having "social lives" or "careers" that are independent of their creators. This section considers Greene's map as a cultural artifact beyond the specific message intended by its author—as an object that embodies multiple layers of signification. This section is a study of the ways the map, as a social artifact, fits into present and future histories (official or otherwise) of Union.

Mrs. Lorna Greene with child, husband (in car), and African American "cook and friend," ca. 1915. Photo courtesy of Peter Greene.

A Material, Written Record

One aspect that makes Greene's map powerful as a statement about Union's past has little to do with the specific contents of the map at all, but rather with the very fact that the statement is made in a map. Ultimately, a map is a material, written record. As such—and regardless of whether or not Mr. Greene had intended this outcome—it is liable to become part of a body of historical knowledge drawn on in the ongoing writing and rewriting of history. In his work on power and the production of history, Michel Rolph Trouillot suggests that "fact creation (the making of sources)" is the first of four moments of history production, and the first in which power imbalance and silences shape historical narratives (1995:26). For a "fact" to be used in the making of histories, it needs, first of all, to exist. That is, the recording of (some) aspect of the past is what produces historical "facts," which are then drawn on in the narration of history. Western historiography has traditionally given primacy to "facts" that are material—and, better yet, written—even though intellectual movements within social and cultural history and historical archaeology have been working to shift this bias.

Perhaps one reason for giving primacy to material, written records is that they reinforce an unspoken tendency to legitimize historical research by making it look like scientific research. Written records promote a scientistic model by pretending to embody qualities that are valued in scientifically oriented studies: transparency and reproducibility. First, written records are tangible: they can be used as "proof" to a challenging audience. Second, they offer a façade of being fixed: their content provides uniform, unchanging "facts" regardless of who the observer may be. Finally, written records appear to be unbiased: a record that was created by an eyewitness, historical actor masquerades as being pure, unfiltered, interpretation-less knowledge (but see Alonso 1988).

The term "primary source" is commonly used by historians to differentiate first hand records that were produced by historical actors from those that are later interpretations. However, an uncritical approach to primary sources conflates their materiality with scientific data, rendering their tangible, fixed, and presumably unbiased characteristics as "primary" in more ways than one. Rather than simply being "original" or "first" records, the term "primary" often suggests that they are also most important or of the highest quality.

As a material, written record, Mr. Greene's map joins an oeuvre of "facts" commonly drawn on and readily recognized as appropriate sources in the writings of history. Even if written records are not always accurate (few historians claim they are) and inherently biased, they are at any rate less ephemeral than oral histories or even material, non-written records (archaeological artifacts, for example). The presence of a written record—concrete, fixed "facts"—is frequently too convenient a source to forfeit in the writing of history, especially if the alternative is an absence of records, or records that are not material or explicit—in other words, the very sort of records that Union's descendant residents produce and share among themselves.

As opposed to the histories narrated by descendant residents, Mr. Greene's map (a late-20th-century document relating a personal reflection about early-20th-century Union) is far more likely to become a resource for future official histories of Union simply because it has a material presence. He reminds his viewers that his map is "not to scale," but neither the temporal distance between the map's creation and the era it is said to represent, nor its choices, omissions, or spatial and temporal distortions are enough to overshadow the fact that a map is a material, written record—a seemingly tangible, fixed, and unbiased "primary" source about the past—and therefore an ideal resource for the writing of official histories.

A Counter-Hegemonic Narrative?

This last point brings us back to the earlier discussion of Greene's map as possibly being conceived as an act of resistance against a state-imposed history of Union. I suggested above that the map drafted by Mr. Greene could be read as a sort of counter-hegemonic statement about Union's past because it offers an opposing vision to that offered in the official NRHP narrative.

The state, represented in this case by the NRHP, sees Union as a historically black community. Mr. Greene, in contrast, represents Union in his map as being singularly white. But while the content of the map may suggest counter-hegemonic discourse, the platform he chose for making his statements certainly does not. It is precisely because "map" means in dominant culture—because it is a material, written record and therefore a primary (and prime) source for history writing—that its counter-hegemonic nature is called into question. The fact that Mr. Greene could so apparently unselfconsciously tap into the dominant culture's modus operandi—producing a written record about Union's past that upholds the notion that such records are indeed primary (tangible, fixed, unbiased)—speaks to his own placement within (rather than against) the dominant culture.

Reproduction

If Ernest Greene had any concerns about the continuing existence of his map as a historical source, they were certainly eased by the creation of multiple copies of it. During the time I conducted fieldwork, I spent many hours in his company and, as mentioned above, was almost always greeted with a pile of material—written records for my safekeeping.

Among these were multiple copies of his map. Like the one I had received in the mail, all were copied onto two large sheets of paper and carefully taped together, but each contained slightly different hand-drawn additions and variations. One map, the first I received, includes the text written by Peter Greene, Ernest's cousin: "Sketched by: Ernest C. Greene about 1998." Another has the line, this time added by Mr. Greene, "Drawn by Ernest Carlton Greene as remembered—1918–1934." Some have additional names added to those already recorded beside each house, several include the river's name at a second location on its course (the river is already named at another point on the original map), and one has lines added to several of the houses representing bird's-eye-view renditions of their roofs.

Like the works of art described by early 20th-century German literary philosopher Walter Benjamin, Greene's hand-drawn map of a memory-scape is a creation that was "designed for reproducibility." The almost-instantaneous act of reproducing the map (an act in which the author himself engages) suggests that this is a case in which "authenticity ceases to be applicable to artistic [or cartographic] production, [and] the total function of art [or mapping] is reversed. . . . [I]t begins to be based on another practice—politics" (1968:224). As I have already suggested, reproducing the map is a way for Mr. Greene to increase the odds that his vision will continue to be represented even after he is gone, ensuring that the map (and by extension his vision of Union) becomes a permanent historical fact.

Each new map, then, is an act of reproduction not only in that a new copy of the original comes into existence, but also because each new "offspring" represents a newly developed history of Union. For Mr. Greene, narrating Union's history is neither a static nor a momentary act, but an ongoing, dynamic, and political re-remembering and re-producing. Rather than leaving his map in its original version as it was drafted in 1998, he creates a series of "base maps" atop which he continues to build. With each new variation of the map, he breathes new life into his narrative about Union's historical landscape, continually tweaking, changing, rendering, customizing.

I personally own three different versions of Greene's map, and I assume that many more exist, circulating or sitting in the archives or attics (or even trash bins) of family members and acquaintances, some likely even in the vaults of local historical societies or libraries—each containing its own set of slight variations and its own reproducible life. I presume that some of the variations in the copies I own were made specifically for my benefit, while other copies may have been customized differently for different viewers. Whatever impressions Mr. Greene wanted to leave with me, a non–family member working on a project that is somehow related to Union's history, might be different perhaps from those that he might want to leave with a grandchild, family friend, or history broker.

Of course, the ongoing making and remaking of Mr. Greene's map points to the fallacy of a material, written record being a scientifically objective "fact" at all. Even a map "in the age of mechanical reproduction" (Benjamin 1968) contains a particular bias—a positionality relative to the terrain it is said to depict—and it can hardly be thought of as "fixed." Mr. Greene's map reminds us that the act of producing history is itself a dynamic remembering of the past, entrenched as much in what about then was chosen to be recorded as in what now are the socio-political dynamics at work. Even a material, written record can be dynamic and interactive, producing a history of space that speaks to current social, political, and economic contexts in which both the cartographer (cum-historian-cum-artist) and his/her audience interact.

Conclusion

I have argued in this chapter that Greene's map can be read as a sort of topographic history of Union, a cartographically communicated narrative about Union's past. Mr. Greene's framing of his map with the words "not to scale" have positioned my own thinking about this cartographic creation in terms of the ways "scale" is employed to shape the map as a historical narrative. The spatial scaling, re-scaling and inter-scaling in Greene's map produce a portrait of his homeplace that reflects his own experiences and interventions. In this portrait, he maps Union as a cohesive, lily-white community, with no clues whatsoever to the presence of black residents.

Greene also tampers with the temporal scale by including perforated-line landmarks atop a solid-lined historical landscape. By recognizing these modern landmarks, contemporary viewers are thus motivated to develop a personal relationship with the terrain depicted on the map—and thereby with the history of a place that is communicated within it. By reproducing multiple copies of the map, Greene ensures that his history of Union will be broadcast at a much larger scale than, for example, the orally transmitted histories told by Union's descendant residents. As someone who cares deeply about official histories and leaving a legacy, he works to ensure not only that his map will have a broad, ongoing, and carefully targeted audience (family, historians, historical archives), but also a fairly good chance of becoming a primary and prime source in future writings of official histories.

Conclusion

Unfolding Communities: Union Road as a "Uniter of People"?

"Why we remember and what we remember, the motive and
the content, are inseparable."
Richard King, *Memory and Phantasy* (1983)

Taken individually, the chapters of this book have offered insights into
particular aspects of the relationships that residents have to community
and by extension to history, space, and race—illuminations that each
group casts on the overlap of these concepts in Union. While some consideration was given in each chapter to the placement of history brokers,
descendant residents, and delegitimized historians within larger social
dynamics, the central aim has been to allow the qualities and internal
logic of each group to be understood and analyzed on its own terms.

Taken together, the chapters form my own rendition of Union, growing out of my experiences with residents and their productions of community, as well as my perspective on the ways history and race map onto a social landscape. Paying close attention to the historical and spatial constructions produced by each group of residents, the previous chapters have endeavored to provide a subtle and intricate reading of the social dynamics that were evolving in the wake of Union's official recognition as a historically black community. Here we broaden the aperture and capture, by way of a conclusion, the ways in which residents' worldviews are influenced by (and sometimes merged with) other people's worldviews in their everyday lives.

Union's various residents—those we have been calling history brokers, descendant residents, and delegitimized historians—do not come into contact with each other in many contexts, but their lives are nonetheless intertwined as they are shaped by many of the same social, political, and economic dynamics. When members of different groups do come together (as, for example, at the annual Union picnic), their interactions leave impressions and continue to inform how members of each group perceive the others. These impressions are subsequently incorporated into residents' own evolving understandings of community. Indeed, the very choice by history brokers to identify Union as historically black space—and later, descendant residents' insistence on having the facts recorded correctly, and the racial re-mapping of Union by a delegitimized historian—are all evidence of residents' dynamic and co-informed relationships to Union as a community.

But how do residents make sense of their neighbors' worldviews and in what ways do they incorporate them into their own relationship to Union? Do descendant residents' concerns with the factual correctness of official histories—despite their emphasis on experiential and fragmented histories in informal settings—mean that they "have been assimilated into a global culture of the present" (Handler 1991:72)? Does Mr. Greene's refusal to acknowledge the presence of African American residents on his map mean that white and black residents are not influenced by each other in a "deep symbiotic relatedness" (Sobel 1987:11)? Were history brokers' efforts to gain official historic recognition for Union motivated solely by a desire to protect their property values?

The answer to all these questions is "no." Union's residents are aware of—and in relationship with—other perspectives of community by which they are surrounded. While the three groups might form distinguishable cultural units, they are also simultaneously part of a wider and jointly produced "global culture of the present." Without diminishing the differences between each group (or their significance), we should be able to recognize that members of the three social resident groups are not living in isolation, but operating within overlapping socio-physical milieus. Residents are all also integral components of the milieus of Union, Piedmont County, Virginia, and indeed the United States—this last one being endlessly diverse, filled with internal contradictions and paradoxes, and transcending simple historical, geographic, or cultural definitions—but which can be said to exist nonetheless, perhaps precisely because of its vast heterogeneity.

The work that people put into thinking about and imagining their community—making sense of and giving context to what they read, hear, see, and experience—creates a unique array of productions of community. While many Union residents may watch television, read the newspaper, or participate in community picnics, the members of each group have very different relationships to what these activities mean, and hence to the nature of the community to which they belong (or, of course, whether they feel like they belong to it in the first place). When residents watch the same local TV news program or read the same newspaper article, they may be "continually reassured that the imagined world is visibly rooted in everyday life" (Anderson 2006:36), but they are also continually engaged in producing unique dialectical relationships with the imagined world in which they operate.

Residents belonging to Union's three main social groups may not come together frequently or in many contexts, but they are still aware of—and influenced by—other residents. The few moments when they do come together offer invaluable insights into this unfolding production of the meanings of community. Such an opportunity presented itself at a June 2002 meeting of the Piedmont County Board of Supervisors. On this occasion Union's residents joined together to support a proposal that would restrict truck traffic on Union Road. The meeting, as well as the events leading up to and resulting from it, were an exercise par excellence in mutually informed productions of community—and by extension, of history, space, and race.

Organized initially by the Union Community Association—but taking on a life of its own—residents drew on the same networks they had established for planning the annual picnics to prepare for this particular meeting of the Piedmont County Board of Supervisors. One UCA member drafted an invitation to attend the meeting, another made photocopies, and several others distributed them to neighbors' mailboxes. Ms. Peters began a "telephone tree," calling some neighbors, asking them to show up for the meeting, and requesting that they pass the word on. Michael Taps called me the day before to ask if "as our resident anthropologist" I could join in for support during the public-hearing portion of the board meeting. According to county regulations, any "member of the public" could sign up to give a three-minute comment during the public-hearing portion—and Michael told me that a group of residents had met "to plan their strategy" for it. The first speaker would "sort of give a tour of the road," Michael explained.

> He's a photographer and he'll talk about different spots and how dangerous they are. Then I'd like to have several people who have local interests— for example, Julia [Peters], one of the Wallace couple, I'm hoping Joanne Mitchell will come to speak, and I'm hoping to get some people from the subdivisions. . . . Then the last two people to speak will be Jack Shifflett and Aaron Chesnick. They'll give the position of the community—and of the Coalition for a Safe Union Road.

In preparation for the meeting, Michael Taps's approach is, perhaps, representative of history brokers' desire to control the shape of events:

history-broker residents are cast as representatives of "the position of the community," while descendants are representative of "local interests." But unlike the unveiling ceremony—in which members of one group of residents (history brokers) had a strong vested interest in the event's outcome, others (descendant residents) were only mildly interested, and others still (delegitimized historians) were left out completely—this event drew keen interest by all residents. The common desire to restrict truck traffic from Union Road, a narrow winding artery that traverses Union, was felt strongly enough by all of Union's residents that an imposed choreography was not only unnecessary but entirely useless.

On the appointed day I arrived at the county office building to find a packed parking lot, a crowded hallway, and residents representing not only the three resident groups discussed in this book, but many others as well, including some who live in the nearby development area but who on this afternoon considered themselves (and were immediately recognized as) part of the Union community. Based on my attendance at innumerable county board meetings throughout the year, I can attest that this recognition was highly unusual.

On normal county board meeting days it was not unusual for me to be the only "member of the public" in the board room, forcing my eyelids to remain open (more out of politeness than intellectual curiosity) as I witnessed tedious discussions about the size of a parking lot at another corner of Piedmont County. But this afternoon was different. There was an excitement in the air—a buzz both heard and felt. Michael Taps moved from one resident to the next, greeting people, urging them to sign up to speak during the public hearing, and trying to orchestrate the order in which we would give our comments. Every new resident who arrived sent the hallway into a hushed but barely contained cacophony: "Bill, you made it!" "Go find Michael and put yourself on the list." "How have you been?" "I tried calling you earlier today."

When the board room opened, we filed in—perhaps 40 of us or more—nearly filling up the rows of chairs designated for "the public." I sat at the edge of the second row beside Joanne Mitchell and Julia Peters.

As I turned to look around the room I found a sea of faces—some familiar, but mostly not—filling the seats around us: William Anderson was there, Michael Taps and Jack Shifflett were there. Our mail carrier came to show his support, and many others whom I later learned lived along Union Road or in nearby subdivisions, or even farther away in the more rural part of the county—but who nonetheless came to support the proposed restriction of trucks on Union Road.

After the county supervisors discussed the proposal on their own for some time—debating in almost academic fashion how one might define "truck" (by weight? number of axles? a combination of the two?) or what constitutes a "viable alternate route"—the floor opened to the public. In all, eight people (including myself) got up to speak, and each of the comments we gave offered insights into the dynamic way we perceive what community is, and how we each think about Union as a community. Three comments in particular, those by subdivision resident Dan Callahan, descendant resident Joanne Mitchell, and history broker resident Jack Shifflett are especially poignant examples for their eclectic use of history and space in articulating Union as a community. The comments of each speaker are reflective of particular understandings of community (and space and history)—but also of the ongoing dialogue within which these understandings exist. Each section begins with an abbreviated version of the comments made by the speaker and is followed by an analysis.

Dan Callahan, Subdivision Resident, Member of Coalition for a Safe Union Road

> Chairman of the board, members of the supervisors. I am Dan Callahan. I live in the Brooks River Subdivision, and I am a member of the Coalition for a Safer Union Road. The Coalition has many concerns with the safety of Union Road. We are particularly concerned with the school . . . which has the capacity of about 600 students. Tonight we're asking you to take a look at one of the concerns that we have—and that is a restriction on through-trucks over two axles between [Routes] 50 and 57. . . . Union Road

historically was the Old Piedmont Road and was established some time back before the Revolutionary War time. The present path follows pretty much the high ground between the north fork and south fork of Mill River, and it is the only solidly paved road that connects those two in northern Piedmont County, except for [Route] 341, which goes across the county line. The Coalition, by the way, has the support of several groups: one, the Union Road Community Association, and the homeowners associations of [he names six subdivisions].The highway is interesting in that it both has an agricultural end at the western end, and on its eastern end it becomes more residential and suburban. . . . We have six subdivisions, we have a shopping center, four churches, one bank, a hospital facility, a lawn and garden store, a lumberyard, a dance studio, and a childcare center. . . . If I describe Union Road to you, it is 5.4 miles long, it contains a total of 41 curves, there is a speed-limit of 45 mph, however there are 12 areas where there are signs asking to reduce the speed, some of them as low as 25 mph. There are 80 of the little triangular signs [chevron alignment signs denoting sharp curves in the road]. . . . Many of the houses are close to the road because they were built before the restriction for a 50-foot setback. Many of the houses on the road are along very curvy road, and lastly we have the Union Road bridge, which is a wooden bridge, a single-lane bridge, that helps us keep the big heavy traffic off of it. But as I said before, a three-axle truck can most easily be seen [and identified] as being in violation. [Having a restriction based on] weight cannot be really taken care of unless they bring a scale. Thank you.

To begin with, the speaker identifies himself as a subdivision resident and a member of the Coalition for a Safer Union Road. Although Union's official Historic District boundaries distinctly exclude the development area, this resident clearly recognizes that experiential boundaries trump official boundaries. In this case the resident, like other residents along Union Road, share the (unpleasant) experience of truck traffic. Indeed, Dan Callahan's comments suggest that his home is part of the Union community: he is part of the Coalition, and he notes that "we have six subdivisions," and "we have the Union Road bridge." Within this "we," Mr. Callahan's home is merely located on the "residential and suburban end" of the road, but is not a separate social unit.

To persuade that trucks should be banned from Union Road, Dan Callahan cites the road's historical significance: it was "established some time back before the Revolutionary War time." He describes its geography: Union Road is "the high ground" between the two forks of a river, is 5.4 miles long, has 41 curves, etc. And he maps the social world brought together by Union Road: "six subdivisions . . . a shopping center, four churches, one bank, a hospital facility, a lawn and garden store, a lumberyard, a dance studio, and a childcare center." Like the visual map drawn by Ernest Greene, Callahan's oral map represents Union Road's sociogeographic terrain in a manner that is designed to drive home a specific point for a particular audience. Concerned with the traffic on Union Road, Callahan's "map" is charted to convince the Board of Supervisors to restrict trucks from the road.

The result is a description reminiscent in its format and language of legitimacy of the NRHP nomination papers. The description offers "factual" statistical and historical data (5.4 miles, 41 curves, 80 alignment signs), invoked to make a convincing case for banning trucks. Like Greene's map (but unlike the NRHP papers), Callahan's comments map Union as a community defined by social relationships, but whose boundaries are tenuous at best. Indeed the physical landscape that he defines as Union is a far cry from the area bounded and defined as the Union Historic District in the nomination papers. Ironically, in drawing on the materials meticulously collected and archived by Union's history brokers (e.g., Union Road's origins), Callahan paints a community that is quite different both in the area it includes and the social networks it represents from that intended by history brokers.

Perhaps the irony is not so cutting. Narratives are formed with a particular audience in mind—and Callahan's intentions are overt. Like most of the people attending the BoS meeting that afternoon, he is interested in improving his quality of life by reducing the amount and type of traffic passing by his home. The words he speaks are intended to represent others who, like himself, are interested in the truck ban, and they were formulated based on the strategy devised by several residents—including some of Union's history brokers.

In concurrence with this strategy, the same sort of language (and indeed some of the very same facts) that history brokers had carefully crafted in order to keep development out of Union were now being employed by a resident of the contentious development area itself in order to jointly call for a truck ban. And while history brokers and the NRHP papers draw boundaries around a community that is epitomized by old homes and black residents, this speaker focuses primarily on the more "residential and suburban" end of the road—the part that lies directly within the development area. Callahan nods towards the homes sitting along Union Road (he mentions that they are close to the road), but offers a map of a place that has a very different essence from the rustic community described in the NRHP nomination papers.

Dan Callahan is aware of the visions of Union articulated by the history brokers, and even incorporates elements into his own narrative, but his comments are not a simple mimicry of the history brokers' understandings of history and space. Instead, they are a reflection of his own relationship to Union as a community. Some of the information he offers draws on the discourse of history brokers, but it is recast and reformulated and made his own.

The comments by Joanne Mitchell present a sharp contrast to this vision.

Joanne Mitchell: Lifelong Resident of Union

Good evening. I am Joanne Gaines Mitchell, resident of Union. I have lived there my entire life. Been away to school and came back. It is a special home and a special neighborhood for me. Not only did I grow up in Union, but some of the very special things about the community are that when I grew up, downtown Union had what we call a country store.

And at that time that's where we actually got our mail. That was before mailboxes were installed in driveways. That was also a place where the community had a Union depot—one could catch a train going north or south and the cost was pennies and quarters. Also, we have in Union the Mt. Zion Baptist Church, which was and is a source of religious and spiritual strength. It still remains there, and I might add that Union has become on the register for historical sites—and we are extremely proud of that. Not only has Union been special, in Union it used to be the norm to walk from one part of the community to the other and not have to worry about visiting or walking on the road. Not that Union is just a community, but to me it also has a lot of history to it. Union was actually started or founded by a former slave, who happens to be a great-great-grandfather of mine. And that makes it even more special. Many of the people who moved into the community see Union for its warmth and caring, and would like to see it remain that way, knowing full well that progress and technology have changed considerably. But the one thing that I am here to say, is that walking on the road or simply driving or coming out of your driveway has become extremely dangerous. There are times where the traffic on Union Road has increased. You will find that vehicles too large and too heavy are approaching you, which means that you often have to move over, or they are already sharing your lane. We also have a one-lane bridge, and we find there, too, that vehicles are too large and too heavy crossing that area as well. If you meet [another vehicle on the road], you have to get over—what you normally have to do is just get to the edge of the road, to the shoulder. Therefore, it seems that we need to remove the large vehicles from traveling on Union Road. That's for safety measures. Not just for walking—but simply driving. Thank you.

Joanne Mitchell describes a community that appears to be defined almost exclusively through its history. Her comments depict Union as the place she remembers from her youth. Mitchell, who is a descendant resident (and the daughter of Jim Gaines), uses her three minutes to portray the quintessential quaint, rustic community that is described in the NRHP narrative. While, importantly, she leaves out any racial component from her description,[1] she paints a romantic landscape of country stores, quiet serenity, welcoming neighbors, and long-lost simplicity—the essentialized community so passionately argued for by history brokers.

There are no hospital facilities or dance studios in Joanne Mitchell's community, no banks or "suburban ends" of the road. In some senses, the map she portrays is similar to the one drawn by Ernest Greene. The landscape through which she carries her audience is a landscape of memory, only gently encroached upon by contemporary anchors—a church that still stands, a bridge on which "too large and too heavy" vehicles should not be allowed to pass.

Most significantly, Mitchell cites Union's official recognition as a Historic District, noting, "we are extremely proud of that." Although for most descendant residents historic recognition came and went without much fanfare, Mitchell notes that she herself is not simply proud, but "extremely proud" of the recognition. The unveiling ceremony may have had its share of problems (it objectified black residents as historical relics and ignored the histories that descendants themselves tell of the place), Mitchell nonetheless picks out elements of the recognition process that she can incorporate into her own unfolding relationship to Union as a community. Her comments combine personal experiences growing up in Union with a sense of pride that emerges because of the place's officially sanctioned history. Historic recognition, after all, was premised on the actions of her own great-great-grandfather.

Besides the real pride that Joanne Mitchell feels for her now canonized ancestors, she also recognizes that in the particular forum in which she is speaking—in front of the county supervisors, and for the purpose of having trucks banned from Union Road—historic recognition also holds considerable clout. Indeed, six years earlier it was county supervisors who voted to move the boundaries of an entire development area away from Union for the very reason of its historic significance. Mitchell, who also participated in the strategy-planning meeting for the truck ban, was responsible for presenting what Michael Taps called the "local interest" angle. As such, her job was to convey to the county supervisors that Union is at its core a quiet rural community that suddenly finds itself tangled in the bustle of urban development.

Joanne Mitchell incorporates into her comments discourse borrowed from history brokers about Union's "founders" and her great-great-grandfather, the "former slave"—even though "founders" and "former slaves" are not labels that her father or other descendants residents tend to employ when narrating histories of Union. Mitchell acknowledges the social cachet that such terms carry, and includes them in her comments. Unlike history brokers, however, the history she presents at the Board of Supervisors meeting does not culminate with Union's slow senescence in the 1940s. While the NRHP papers cite the closing of the general merchandise store and train depot as signs of Union's decline as a community, Joanne Mitchell's narrative describes a community defined through family and social ties, not economic vitality. The continuum which begins with her great-great-grandfather is maintained still, as evidenced by her continued residence in Union.

While history brokers' discourse suggests that the Union community will somehow be saved in part as a result of historical recognition, Mitchell's comments describe an already existing and viable community that welcomes new residents through the show of "warmth and caring." "Progress and technology" may have changed the nature of the community, but there is no sense in her comments that community has in any way been threatened or diminished by change. Although her comments are shaped by the discourse of history brokers, Mitchell does not simply assimilate their perspective. Rather, her comments are a thoughtful reassessment of her own relationship to the community (expressed in terms of experiences and stories about her ancestors) in light of what outsiders seem to find interesting about it.

The integration of Joanne Mitchell's sense of the community with how others perceive the community configures somewhat differently in the discourse of history broker Jack Shifflett:

Jack Shiflett, Resident and Member of the
Coalition for a Safe Union Road

Madam Chairman, members of the board, my name is Jack Shifflett. I reside on Union Road and have been there for 18 years. I, too, am a member of the Coalition for a Safe Union Road and urge you to support the ban on through-trucks on Union Road between [Routes] 50 and 57. We are proud of our neighborhood and concerned for its future. We understand progress, but we want it to reflect our values, and our concept of the future. We are proud that over 300 people agree with us and signed our petition in our neighborhood. Safety should be the primary consideration for any road that handles residential, commuter, commercial, and school-bus traffic. It is our contention that removing one element from the mix will make the road safer for others. The staff report took an in-depth look at our proposal and agreed with us on three of the five criteria, namely: Alternative, Function, and Design. If you count school enrollment at 600 pupils, surely the Density requirement will be met also, making four of the five. On balance, we think that the staff did a fair review of our requests and reached the logical conclusion. . . . With the beginning of the school year this fall we feel that the timing [for banning trucks] would be excellent for both parties. We recognize that the ban in no way affects businesses on Union Road. We look to the future and see a road that serves as a main street to our community. A uniter of people and not a sword that cuts a path through us and divides us. And so on behalf of more than 300 residents of the Union area, and in the name of 600 little children, we ask you to approve this ban. . . . With your indulgence, Madam Chairman, I'd like to ask all those in the audience from our neighborhood who support us to stand up. [Everyone in the audience rises.]

According to the strategy, Jack Shifflett was supposed to be the last scheduled member of the public to speak that evening. Though he was followed by three more speakers who spontaneously decided to voice their support of the truck ban, Shifflett's speech was designed as a grand finale for the comments voiced "by the community." "We are proud of our neighborhood," he declares, and "proud that over 300 people agree with us." His comments are not intended as a personal anecdote, as were those offered by Joanne Mitchell, or even to some extent those by Dan Callahan. Rather they are a record of "our values and our concept of the future."

Jack Shifflett's comments were presented in a tone that is authoritative and rather official, but also embellished with a conscious hint of small-town living. Like Joanne Mitchell's comments, Shifflett's goal too is to paint Union as a community that is cohesive, that shares a set of values, and that is made up of individuals who care for one another. The social unit that Jack describes reflects this image: it is not a road but a neighborhood—a unit that denotes a small and familiar, close-knit social space.[2]

Like Joanne Mitchell, Jack Shifflett too invokes the idea of "progress" but in a significantly different context. Mitchell describes progress as having "changed our community." Progress in her comments does not denote values, but an external and apparently superficial change that happened to the community. In Shifflett's comments, on the other hand, progress is portrayed as an almost inevitable evil—something that must be dealt with but that, with the right group of people, can be reined in and properly controlled so that it reflects "our" values.

Although throughout the process of obtaining historic recognition by the NRHP, Union's history brokers left themselves out of the narrative, speaking as objective newcomer outsiders rather than "native" Union-ites who are part of the community, at this moment Jack Shifflett represents himself—and every one of the 300 residents who signed the petition—as every bit insiders, every bit "natives," every bit part of the community and therefore justified in having an opinion that needs to be reflected in the future of "our neighborhood." The 18 years in which Shifflett had lived in Union were no longer a mark of his status as outsider, as they were in the process of writing Union's NRHP narrative. Instead, these years became a mark of his investment in the place as a home, his very insider-hood in the community.

The dramatic conclusion to Jack Shifflett's remarks represents his own map of Union—a map that, like Mitchell's comments, suggests a close-knit social space, but which, unlike Mitchell, intimates that this rustic community is under threat of being "slain" by the road. While in Dan Callahan's comments, Union Road was a synonym for the community (a connector between people and places of business), in Shifflett's comments the road should be a "uniter of people" but instead is now a "sword that cuts a path through us and divides us." For added effect, Shifflett notes the existence of a nearby school and the "600 little children" in whose name also he implores the supervisors to place a ban on trucks.

Union's history brokers frequently speak both in public and in private about Union as "our community" and the strong sense of belonging they feel for the place. But the manner in which social, economic, and primarily racial differences are erased in Jack Shifflett's comments were novel. There is a sense in his comments—and indeed in all the comments that evening—that Union is not a home to descendant residents, history brokers, or delegitimized historians, not a place where "black" or "white" residents live, but a community, a neighborhood, a social space in which people jointly rally to support a common cause. Jack Shifflett invokes descendant residents' discourse about the community, but revamps it to include all of Union's residents, including himself, as part of this unified social world. Joanne Mitchell paints the community through experiences from her youth, but does so in a way that emphasizes Union as a "special" (and race-less) community of which all current (and race-less) residents can be proud. Dan Callahan tampers with the boundaries of the Historic District to depict Union as a community defined by a particular historical narrative, but also unproblematically includes both the official Union Historic District and nearby subdivisions.

There was an electric feeling in the room when we all stood up on Jack Shifflett's cue. I looked around and observed that every person in the audience was standing, including people who came to observe the meeting for unrelated reasons. The supervisors looked on with broad smiles: this is precisely the kind of community they like to imagine populates their county—a group of people whom the state identifies as sharing a single geographical affiliation (all residents of Union), and who in turn internalize this identity and reflect it back by representing themselves to the supervisors as members of a (single) community. To ensure that they were not missing any dissenting voices, the chairwoman asked if anyone else would like to speak. Three people rose, all overcoming initial apprehensions about public speaking to add their voices in support of the truck ban. In a few short moments the hearing was over—the Supervisors unanimously voted to have trucks over two axles permanently banned from Union Road.

We poured out of the room in much the same manner as we had originally poured in—but this time our excitement could not be quelled. We stood in the hallway for over an hour chattering energetically, first about the hearing itself, and when some of the exhilaration wore off, about whatever topics happened to arise. Twice representatives from the board room came out to ask us to quiet down, until finally we moved as a cluster to another part of the building. Indeed, standing in the hallway we were a community that for once exhibited close social networks, shared social values, and a single physical location. Joanne Mitchell was dragged off for a short while by a local radio reporter who wanted "sound bites" for a news item on the hearing. Dan Callahan passed around photos he had taken of Union Road, which he presented during the hearing. The photos captured primarily "reduced speed limit" road signs and danger-ous curves, but the story of each image was nonetheless followed with lively social interactions.

The conversations outside the board room represented a moment of unity and solidarity that cut across economic and racial divisions in a way I had not seen before. My own understanding of the concept of "community" was being performed—for one of the few times jointly by all of Union's residents present at the meeting. A young couple shyly told us that they had recently moved to Union. They had bought an old house on Union Road and had already begun restoring it—a project they were planning to do entirely on their own. Mr. Anderson, who always appreciates folks who "are not afraid to work," immediately struck up a conversation with the husband. They soon discovered that both men were plumbers and fell into a long conversation about plumbing projects and exchanging tips of the trade. Ms. Peters stood in a group with several other residents whom I did not know, each relating frightening experiences they had had with speeding trucks on Union Road. Some of the older residents reminisced about the various incarnations of the County office building in which we were currently standing.

Eventually we dispersed, but still with an empowered sense of community that was produced during the meeting. The truck ban itself was merely a catalyst for a rare moment in which residents were indeed producing and experiencing "the Union community" in a form that was quite noticeably lacking during my fieldwork. Here at the Board of Supervisors meeting was an array of residents who, in a rare coming together, were able to demonstrate (to themselves as much as to the supervisors) shared values, cohesiveness, and networks that to some extent correspond to a physical landscape in a moment of unity when social divisions are truly unimportant.

Conclusion

The moment of euphoria faded quickly, of course. Residents drove home and returned to their own economic and racial circles with little contact with one another. The supervisors' meeting became a memory that is now sometimes invoked as evidence of the "community" that is said to exist in Union, though most residents still only come together as a group once a year during the annual picnic. But even if this event was an anomaly, the meeting gave an opportunity to observe the ongoing production and experience of community in Union as well as residents' evolving and mutually produced relationship to history, space, and race.

Union became officially recognized as a Historic District in 1999. Each of Union's various residents—members of the three groups described in this book and many others who also consider themselves residents of

Jim Gaines, telling stories at his home. Photo by John Edwin Mason.

Union—had a relationship to official historic recognition and it influenced their understandings of Union as a community. For Ernest Greene, community was defined primarily through social networks that had a relationship (though flexible) to the landscape. Historic recognition encouraged Mr. Greene to draw a racially exclusive map, a sort of spatial negative of the social landscape presented in the NRHP narrative. For Joanne Mitchell, community similarly emerged from social networks linked to physical space. For her, historic recognition came to frame her own historical narratives in the context of what she believes makes the community "special." For Jordan Lawson, the Community Association's vice president, community was first a physical landscape from which social relationships would emerge. For him, historic recognition meant that although he identified as a white man he could feel pride in being part of a historically black community. Each of the residents' experiences and productions of community incorporated new layers of signification as a result of historic recognition—and these continue to evolve and unfold as the residents (and former residents) continue to have social interactions with the world around them.

It would be easy—but inaccurate—as suggested in the introduction to this book, to claim that history brokers are interested only in furthering their own goals regardless of the hopes and expectations of descendant residents; that descendants are simply victims of an oppressive power structure whose own narratives are silenced; or that delegitimized historians' feeling of marginalization is nothing but a figment of their imagination. In negotiating the dynamic and shifting relationship between the physical landscape and the social networks that exist within it, residents are involved in producing meaning, incorporating new knowledge into their experiences and productions of community, and are continually balancing what they hear, see, and experience with what they believe the world to be.

NOTES

NOTES TO CHAPTER 1

1. As noted in the acknowledgments, the names of the people described in this ethnography have been changed in respect of their privacy. For the same reason, the names of "Union" and related sites have been changed as well.

2. The social tragedy in the wake of Hurricane Katrina's devastation of the U.S. Gulf Coast (August 2005) is one clear example of how closely history, space, and race are glossed in popular imagination. As many will recall, the appallingly poor preparation for the hurricane and the slow response in its aftermath sparked a national debate about the racist undertones of the government's actions (or lack of action). The hurricane also highlighted the deep chasm between "haves" and "have-nots" in the United States, chasms that almost inevitably trace racial lines. Poverty, lack of opportunity, and poor access to basic resources were all exposed as part of the daily experiences of many Americans—and predominantly the domain of African Americans. New Orleans, which was the focus of media coverage during and after the hurricane, continues to be imagined (and portrayed) as a black space, and the federal government's failure to respond was read by many not only as a blatant contemporary act of racism, but also the child of a long legacy of black disenfranchisement in the United States.

3. Benedict Anderson's well-known discussion of the origins of national identity (Imagined Communities 2006) is, of course, a seminal work in the literature that focuses explicitly on history, space, and race, even if Anderson himself does not use these terms. Instead, the author describes the census, the map, and the museum as "three institutions of power . . . [that] profoundly shaped the way in which the colonial state imagined its dominion—the nature of the human beings it ruled, the geography of its domain, and the legitimacy of its ancestry" (167–68). Writing in the discipline of political science, Anderson's findings focus on the state's imaginings of "its dominion." My own work attempts to probe the dialectic between state imaginings and those of the "dominion" itself: men and women who live their lives within and through state-defined categories.

4. The distinction I make between history and the past—well delineated by German's differentiation of *historie* and *geschichte*—grows out of a broad body of work theorizing the difference between the *past* and *narratives* about the past. Most directly, I draw on Lévi-Strauss's distinction between "historical fact" and

"history-for" (1966:257–58), de Certeau's distinction between "history" and "historiography" (1988:xxvii), and Trouillot's distinction between "historicity 1" ("what happened") and "historicity 2" ("what was said to have happened") (1995). While the Spanish term *historia* refers both to fictional narratives ("stories") and narratives about the past ("histories"), in English the term "history" glosses the past and narratives told *about* the past. In this book I use "history" to refer only to narratives about the past.

5. The names I use to refer to Union's residents correspond to the way I was introduced to them and how I eventually came to refer to them. I write of Julia Peters, for example, as "Ms. Peters," but Celia Marshall was known to most as "Ms. Celie." Likewise, Jordan Lawson and Pauline Coles both asked that I call them by their first names—naming practices that I reflect in my writing.

6. These numbers are approximations because Union is not identified as a distinct unit by the U.S. Census Bureau, and therefore no aggregate information is available about it. Information about individual households (which I could then potentially aggregate myself) is not made public until 70 years after it has been collected. The data here are therefore based on my own research, drawing on an admittedly imperfect apparatus, and also reflecting my personal bias about what should or should not be included within Union's boundaries.

7. The term "training schools" was a euphemism for institutions (such as the one attended by Union's black children in the 1930s, 1940s, and 1950s) in which African Americans were taught "industrial education" or "practical training." "In the name of progress and educational change, reformers, under the rubric of 'industrial' education, advocated inaugurating a segregated pedagogy that sanctioned substantial inequalities," writes William Link (1986:177). In real terms, these schools taught African American children skills that specifically prepared them to enter the workforce as farm laborers and domestic servants.

8. The Civilian Conservation Corps (CCC) was a national program instituted in the 1930s by Franklin D. Roosevelt as part of his public works program. Young men were recruited and deployed around the country in "forest works" projects. The creation of the nearby Shenandoah National Park was one such project (for the controversies surrounding this project, see Martin-Perdue 1983; Perdue and Martin-Perdue 1991). Jim Gaines, a descendant resident, was a CCC recruit.

NOTES TO CHAPTER 2

1. In a memorable flare-up of public debate over the nature of history and historicity, British historian David Irving was sentenced in February 2006 to three years in prison "for denying the Holocaust." The trial, which took place in Austria, offers an excellent window into the fierce emotions prompted by history telling, the state's deep desire to keep historical narratives static, and the inherent futility of such an endeavor. In this case, the Austrian state pronounces quite clearly its desire to fix history: Reuters reports that in Austria "denying the Nazi genocide

is a crime punishable by one to ten years in jail." And yet Irving articulates
the fundamental contradiction of history as a static narrative by stating in his
defense that "history is a constantly growing tree—the more you know, the more
documents become available, the more you learn, and I have learnt a lot since
1989" (Reuters UK Online, "Irving Says No Longer Denies Holocaust," Feb. 20,
2006). In response to the accusation that his changed perspective was "only a
pretense . . . in order to escape jail time" (Irving had said in court that he changed
his views and the Holocaust did indeed occur), he retorted, "Any sane historian is
going to be entitled to open this package that the media describe as the Holocaust
and look at the individual contents and say "well, this part I believe and this part I
believe and most of that I believe but there is one thing here I don't believe. . . . It
is not so much of a change of heart, it is just a refining of your position" (Reuters
UK Online, "I Won't Be Silenced, Says Irving," posted Feb. 22, 2006).

2. As an example of the "language of historic legitimation," consider NRHP's
   description of the local church: "A more intact reminder of [Union]'s black heritage is the [Mt. Zion] Baptist Church, an excellent vernacular Gothic Revival-style
   church built in 1891, located at the south end of the district" (page 1). Here, the
   authors combine their training in architectural history with an understanding
   that certain architectural formations serve as a sort of signature for a particular
   time period (in a specific region). The descriptor "vernacular Gothic Revival-
   style" allows the authors to cleverly "remind" NRHP reviewers that the building—
   and by extension, the community to which it belongs—conforms to an existing
   knowledge base, that the church is, in fact, an "excellent" example, and therefore
   should be worthy of historic recognition.

3. Whether one perceives such historical texts to represent true or legendary events
   is irrelevant to the fact that the text is believed to be historical—representing
   events from the past.

4. The NRHP defines "historic" properties as those "significant in American history,
   archeology, architecture, engineering, or culture."

5. Subdivisions are planned housing developments that are created by partitioning
   large properties (in Piedmont County these are usually former plantations) into
   much smaller lots. A single development company usually purchases the entire
   lot with an agreement that the homes will all be built within a designated amount
   of time and will adhere to a single aesthetic, giving the planned community a
   stylistically homogeneous look.

NOTES TO CHAPTER 3

1. For another example of a formal and informal history narrated by Jim Gaines, see
   Brand 2007.

2. I use the term "adoptive kinship" to describe social relationships that, while not
   biologically based, functioned in the same manner as consanguinal or affinal
   kinship relations. So, for example, Louise Coles was a granddaughter to Celia

Marshall as much as any of her other grandchildren, even though the two were not biologically related. Louise was Ms. Celie's granddaughter because Louise's mother (Regina Anderson) was raised by Celia and Benjamin Marshall. And since Ms. Celie herself grew up in the home of her adoptive great-uncle, she was effectively a cousin to Jim Gaines, who was raised by the uncle's brother. Louise, then, was Jim Gaines's great-uncle's grandniece's daughter's daughter—or, in local parlance, "kin," regardless of the absence of biological or legal ties.

3. At one point Mr. Gaines was overpowered by the emotional life of the memory, saying that his wife "went crazy" and "took it so hard," but he quickly reestablished the descriptive format, noting that "we didn't have nothing left."

4. The women who helped care for Mr. Gaines while I was doing fieldwork—his daughter, his neighbor Ms. Julia Peters, and eventually also myself—were familiar with the term that Mr. Gaines used for invoking memories of his grandmother. We knew also of the tough disciplinarian upbringing she imparted and we sometimes invoked it ourselves when Mr. Gaines was not doing as he should: "Jeems, you staying out of trouble, Jeems?" his daughter would ask as she entered his house. Or I, taking my cue from the other women, would seal a commitment as I would prepare to leave his home: "I know you're gonna do those exercises your doctor said. . . . Right, Jeems?"

NOTES TO CHAPTER 4

1. For an illuminating discussion of historical sources and narratives—and the production of history in general—see Trouillot 1995 (also White 1978; Appadurai 1981; Alonso 1988; de Certeau 1988; Herzfeld 1991).

2. "A place in history" (a concept borrowed from Herzfeld 1991, but reworked somewhat differently in this section) denotes in this context at least three possible interpretations of this expression: (1) the potential for the map to be consulted in the production of future historical narratives (official or otherwise); (2) the inclusion of Mr. Greene himself as the map's cartographer in the annals of Union's history; and (3) a continuous and ongoing claim to a particular place—Union—over the course of time.

3. Recognizing the problematic connotations of the word "natural," I use the term with caution. Here, "natural" refers to elements in the landscape that exist without the assistance or contribution of humans—regardless of the fact (which I accept) that our understanding of these elements is socially mitigated.

4. A racially intermixed layout of homes is not, in fact, unique to Union nor (clearly) is it indicative of racially intermixed social interactions. Rather, this kind of "mixed" geography is a relatively common feature of rural communities in Virginia. Even though the crippling effects of Jim Crow segregation certainly did not skip over rural communities such as Union, I have heard from both black and white residents that the apartheid-like spatial segregation and ghettoization often associated with the Jim Crow era was prevalent mostly in urban, not rural,

settlements. Nonetheless, as this map clearly indicates, Union's black and white residents were still living in distinctly segregated worlds, even if their houses happened to be intermingled.

5. Residents in Union raised enough food to take care of most of their own needs, but still bought some basic products in the store—and at any rate were dependent on non-agricultural employment for their livelihood.

NOTES TO THE CONCLUSION

1. Joanne Mitchell does point out that the place was founded by a "former slave" who was a "great-great-grandfather of mine," and though slavery in the United States does imply blackness, she does not emphasize this point. The great-great-grandfather's social personhood (former slave) already bespeaks racial identity, but her comments focus instead on the kind of lifestyle in which she remembers participating in Union.

2. When the Union Community Association first formed, it was named the Union Neighborhood Association. Only after several years was the suggestion made to replace the word "neighborhood" with "community." The resident who made the suggestion, a delegitimized historian who rarely attends UCA meetings (but whose wife was an active member of the organization), explained that "neighborhoods are in cities, and we live in the country." The explanation immediately jibed with the image of Union that history brokers want to portray, and the change was made permanent.

BIBLIOGRAPHY

Alonso, Ana Maria. 1988. "The Effect of Truth: Re-Presentations of the Past and the
Imagining of Community." Journal of Historical Sociology 1(1):33–57.

Amit, Vered, ed. 2002. Realizing Community: Concepts, Social Relationships and
Sentiments. London: Routledge.

Anderson, Benedict. 2006. Imagined Communities: Reflections on the Origin and
Spread of Nationalism. New Edition. London: Verso.

Appadurai, Arjun. 1981. "The Past as a Scarce Resource." Man, the Journal of the Royal
Anthropological Institute 16(2):201–19.

———. 1996. "Consumption, Duration, and History." In Modernity at Large: Cultural
Dimensions of Globalization. Minneapolis: University of Minnesota Press.

———, ed. 1988. The Social Life of Things: Commodities in Cultural Perspective. Cambridge, UK: Cambridge University Press.

Appleby, Joyce, Lynn Hunt, and Margaret Jacob. 1994. Telling the Truth About History.
New York: W. W. Norton & Company.

Bachelard, Gaston. 1994[1958]. The Poetics of Space: The Classic Look at How We
Experience Intimate Places. Maria Jolas, trans. Boston: Beacon Press.

Benjamin, Walter. 1968[1955]. Illuminations. Hannah Arendt, ed. Harry Zohn, trans.
New York: Schocken Books.

Blakely, Edward J., and Mary Gail Snyder. 1997. Fortress America: Gated Communities
in the United States. Washington, D.C.: Brookings Institution Press and Lincoln
Institute of Land Policy.

Borofsky, Robert. 2000. Remembrance of Pacific Pasts: An Invitation to Remake History. Hawaii: University of Hawaii Press.

Brand, Mieka. 2007. "Making Moonshine: Thick Histories in a U.S. Historically Black
Community." Anthropology and Humanism 32(1):52–61.

Caldeira, Teresa. 2000. City of Walls: Crime, Segregation, and Citizenship in São
Paulo. Berkeley: University of California Press.

Calvino, Italo. 1974[1972]. Invisible Cities. William Weaver, trans. San Diego: Harcourt Press.

Casey, Edward S. 2002. Representing Place: Landscape Painting and Maps. Minneapolis: University of Minnesota Press.

de Certeau, Michel. 1988[1975]. The Writing of History. Tom Conley, trans. New York:
Columbia University Press.

Cohen, Anthony P. 1985. The Symbolic Construction of Community. London: Tavistock.

Delanty, Gerard. 2009. Community: Second Edition (Key Ideas). London and New York: Routledge.

Douglas, Mary. 1984[1966]. Purity and Danger: An Analysis of the Concepts of Pollution and Taboo. London and New York: Routledge.

Durkheim, Émile. 2008[1912]. The Elementary Forms of Religious Life (Oxford World Classics). Carol Cosman, trans. Oxford and New York: Oxford University Press.

Geertz, Clifford. 1973. "Thick Description: Toward an Interpretive Theory of Culture." In The Interpretation of Cultures: Selected Essays by Clifford Geertz. New York: Basic Books.

Handler, Richard. 1991. "Who Owns the Past? History, Cultural Property, and the Logic of Possessive Individualism." In The Politics of Culture. Brett Williams, ed. Pp. 63–74. Washington, D.C.: Smithsonian Institute Press.

Harley, J. B. 1988. "Silences and Secrecy: The Hidden Agenda of Cartography in Early Modern Europe." Imago Mundi 40:57–76.

———. 2001. The New Nature of Maps: Essays in the History of Cartography. Paul Laxton, ed. Baltimore: Johns Hopkins University Press.

Herzfeld, Michael. 1991. A Place in History: Social and Monumental Time in a Cretan Town. Princeton: Princeton University Press.

Higginbotham, Evelyn Brooks. 1992. "African American Women's History and the Metalanguage of Race." Signs: Journal of Women in Culture and Society 17(2):251–74.

Horst, Heather A., and Mieka Brand, eds. 2008. "Gating Communities" (special issue). Home Cultures 5(1).

Hurston, Zora Neale. 1990[1935]. Mules and Men. New York: Harper Perennial.

King, Richard. 1983. "Memory and Phantasy." Modern Language Notes 98(5):1197–213.

Labov, William, and Joshua Waletzky. 1967. "Narrative Analysis: Oral Versions of Personal Experience." In Essays on the Verbal and Visual Arts. Proceedings of the 1966 Annual Spring Meeting of the American Ethnological Society. June Helm, ed. Pp. 12–44. Seattle and London: University of Washington Press.

Lefebvre, Henri. 1991[1974]. The Production of Space. Donald Nicholson-Smith, trans. Oxford: Blackwell Publishing.

Lévi-Strauss, Claude. 1966[1962]. The Savage Mind. Chicago: University of Chicago Press.

Link, William A. 1986. A Hard Country and a Lonely Place: Schooling, Society, and Reform in Rural Virginia, 1870–1920. Chapel Hill and London: University of North Carolina Press.

Low, Setha M. 2001. "The Edge and the Center: Gated Communities and the Discourse of Urban Fear." American Anthropologist 103(1):45–58.

———. 2003. Behind the Gates: Life, Security, and the Pursuit of Happiness in Fortress America. New York and London: Routledge.

Martin-Perdue, Nancy J. 1983. "Clouds over the Blue Ridge." Commonwealth: The Magazine of Virginia (May):59–63.

Molho, Anthony, and Gordon S. Wood, eds. 1998. Imagined Histories: American Historians Interpret the Past. Princeton: Princeton University Press.

National Register of Historic Places (NRHP). 1993. "My Property Is Important to American Heritage, What Does That Mean? Answers to Questions for Owners of Historic Properties." By Beth L. Savage and Marilyn Harper. http://www.cr.nps.gov/ nr/publications/bulletins/myproperty (accessed July 29, 2012).

———. 1998. Nomination papers submitted in connection for the [Union] Historic District (unpublished).

Organization for a Sustainable Population (OSP). N.d. Informational brochure of the OSP (unpublished).

Perdue, Charles L., Jr., and Nancy J. Martin-Perdue. 1991. "'To Build a Wall Around These Mountains': The Displaced People of Shenandoah." Magazine of Albemarle County History 49:49–71.

Peristiany, J. G., ed. 1966. Honor and Shame: The Values of Mediterranean Society. Chicago: University of Chicago Press.

[Piedmont County]. 1995. Planning Commission Minutes, November 21, 1995 ("PC 11/21").

———. 1995. Planning Commission Minutes, December 19, 1995 ("PC 12/19").

———. 1996. Comprehensive Plan/Land Use Plan section ("Comp Plan").

Pitt-Rivers, Julian. 1966. "Honor and Social Status." In Honor and Shame: The Values of Mediterranean Society. J. G. Peristiany, ed. Chicago: University of Chicago Press.

———. 1968. "Honor." In International Encyclopedia of the Social Sciences, Volume 6. David L. Sills, ed. New York: Macmillan and Free Press.

Price, Richard. 2002. First Time: The Historical Vision of an Afro-American People. Chicago and London: University of Chicago Press.

Redfield, Robert. 1956. The Little Community and Peasant Society and Culture. Chicago: University of Chicago Press.

Reuters UK Online. 2006. "Austria Sentences Irving to Jail for Holocaust Denial." By Mark Heinrich. February 20, 2006.

———. 2006. "Irving Says No Longer Denies Holocaust." By Mark Heinrich. February 20, 2006.

———. 2006. "I Won't Be Silenced, Says Irving." February 26, 2006.

Rosaldo, Renato. 1980. Ilongot Headhunting 1883–1974: A Study in Society and History. Stanford: Stanford University Press.

Sahlins, Marshall. 1981. Historical Metaphors and Mythical Realities: Structure in Early History of the Sandwich Islands Kingdom. Ann Arbor: University of Michigan Press.

———. 1985. Islands of History. Chicago: University of Chicago Press.

Schneider, Jane, and Rayna Rapp, eds. 1995. Articulating Hidden Histories: Exploring the Influence of Eric R. Wolf. Berkeley: University of California Press.

Shaw, Rosalind. 2002. Memories of the Slave Trade: Ritual and the Historical Imagination in Sierra Leone. Chicago and London: University of Chicago Press.

Sobel, Mechal. 1987. The World They Made Together: Black and White Values in Eighteenth-Century Virginia. Princeton: Princeton University Press.

Soja, Edward W. 1989. Postmodern Geographies: The Reassertion of Space in Critical Social Theory. London and New York: Verso.

Stewart, Kathleen. 1996. A Space on the Side of the Road: Cultural Poetics in an "Other" America. Princeton: Princeton University Press.

Tönnies, Ferdinand. 2001[1887]. Community and Civil Society (Gemeinschaft und Gesellschaft). Jose Harris, ed. Jose Harris and Margaret Hollis, trans. Cambridge, UK: Cambridge University Press.

Trouillot, Michel Rolph. 1995. Silencing the Past: Power and the Production of History. Boston: Beacon Press.

Tuan, Yi-Fu. 2002[1977]. Space and Place: The Perspective of Experience. Minneapolis: University of Minnesota Press.

Turner, Victor. 1970. The Forest of Symbols. Ithaca: Cornell University Press.

———. 1975. Dramas, Fields and Metaphors: Symbolic Action in Human Society. Ithaca: Cornell University Press.

———. 1995[1969]. The Ritual Process: Structure and Anti-Structure. Piscataway: Aldine Transaction.

U.S. Department of the Interior, National Park Service (NPS). 2012. National Register of Historic Places Registration Form. NPS Form 10-900.

Virginia Commonwealth. 1975. Code of Virginia, Title 15.2, Chapter 22, § 2223 "Comprehensive Plan to Be Prepared and Adopted; Scope and Purpose."

White, Hayden. 1978. "The Burden of History." In Tropics of Discourse: Essays in Cultural Criticism. Pp. 27–50. Baltimore and London: Johns Hopkins University Press.

Wolf, Eric R. 1982. Europe and the People Without History. Berkeley: University of California Press.

INDEX

Adderly, Margaret, 11, 13, 16-17, 19, 21
African-American, 28, 71, 83, 133, 148; educational options, 29; families, 134; histories, 71, 75-76, 83; homes, 130-131, 135; labor, 8-9, 31, 34, 92, 96, 105; property ownership, 8-9. *See also* community
African-American Heritage Trail, 54
Anderson, Benedict, 167n3
Anderson, Regina (resident), 11, 13-16, 30, 170n2
Anderson, William (resident), 11, 19, 79, 95-100, 100-105, 107, 113, 152, 162
Appadurai, Arjun, 24, 32, 139, 170n1
architectural history, 48, 49, 169n2; Gothic Revival, 169n2
army, 29, 37-38, 138
authenticity, 27, 41, 49, 58, 143

Bachelard, Gaston, 53, 115, 119
Benjamin, Walter, 143-144
blackness, 4, 69, 171n1
built environment as historical record, 26, 31

Callahan, Dan (subdivision resident), 152-155, 160-162
Calvino, Italo, 1-2
cartography, 41, 115-145; cartographer, 144, 170n2; cartographically disenfranchised, 133-135
census, 33, 130, 167n2, 168n6

Certeau, Michel de, 168n4, 170n1
Chesnick, Aaron, 150
child rearing and disciplining, 93-94, 111-113, 170n4
childhood in Union, 29, 36, 111; experiences of children, 29, 105-107, 111, 121
Christianity, 56, 79
church, 9, 29, 34, 41, 54, 79, 82, 88, 91, 94, 110-111, 127, 154, 157; Calvary Christian Church, 120, 122, 126; Mt. Tabor Baptist Church, 118, 122, 130; Mt. Zion Baptist Church, 5, 53-56, 68, 117-118, 130-133, 156, 169n2
Civil Rights Movement, 102-103
Civil War, 7-8, 35-38, 66, 121, 124, 134, 137; Confederate army, 37, 138; Confederate paraphernalia, 38; General Custer, 124; heroes, 37; soldiers, 37-38, 68, 136-137; Union army, 38; winning and losing, 37, 38
Civilian Conservation Corps (CCC), 29, 168n8
Coalition for a Safe Union Road, 149-150, 152
Coles, Louise, 90, 100, 105-107, 168n5, 169n2, 170n2
community, 2-4, 15, 28, 40, 42, 57, 95, 116, 171n2; accumulation of social relationships, 57; African-American, 20, 28, 59, 73-74, 130, 133; as concept, 2-4, 42-45, 171n2;

Harley, J. B., 115, 121, 134-135
Herzfeld, Michael, 170n1, 170n2
hidden histories, 83
historians/researchers (lay and
    professional), 11-27, 32-43, 48, 50-51, 62,
    67, 71, 74-76, 83-84, 137, 145, 169n1
historic highway marker, 4, 40-41, 48-49,
    52, 57, 59-60, 68
historic preservation, funding for, 54
historic vs. historical, 60
historical sensibilities, 47
historical societies, 137, 144
historically black community, concept,
    3-4, 7, 10; politics and power dynamics
    of, 42, 48, 52, 119, 135; Union, 2-4, 7, 10,
    19-20, 26, 33, 42, 46-49, 59, 61, 74, 116,
    119, 122, 135, 138, 142, 148, 164
historicity, 4, 6, 12, 15, 47, 168n1
historic-ness, 6, 30, 47, 50-51, 54, 61, 81,
    104. *See also* Union, historic-ness of
histories: alternative narratives, 38, 51, 72,
    75-76, 81, 85, 89, 92, 95, 138; embedded
    in conversations about the present, 14,
    76, 78, 81, 84-85, 100, 113; in everyday
    discussion, 36, 82, 84; formal vs.
    informal narratives, 41, 75-76, 84, 87,
    89-90, 92-95, 99-100, 114, 169n1, 170n3;
    fragments, 41, 76-80, 99, 108-114, 148;
    multiplicity of, 12, 15, 38, 47, 51, 62, 72,
    75, 81, 95, 96, 99, 108, 144; narration/
    writing/telling of, 15-16, 25, 33, 36,
    41, 50, 59, 61, 76, 81-82, 121, 168n1;
    in relation to the present, 78, 84, 95,
    100, 113-114, 120-121; repetition of, 78,
    81, 85, 95-100, 113-114; temporality,
    100-105, 107-108, 129. *See also* African-
    American: histories; history
history, 25; as anecdote, 104; anticipated
    vs. unanticipated reading, 82; archives/
    records, 10- 11, 26, 31, 36, 49, 84, 90,
    140, 145, 154; books and documents,
    121, 124-125, 136; data/sources, 62, 66,

121, 125, 127-128, 170n1; demonstrating
the strength of the community,
107; dispossession of, 37, 116; as
dynamic narrative about the past,
144, 169n1; as essence of Union, 26,
157; as ethnographic invention, 82;
experiential, 148; facts, 12, 14-15, 26, 36,
75-76, 82, 94, 121, 140-141, 143-144, 148,
154-155; in flux, 47-48; forgetting, 91; as
form of sociality, 15, 16-17, 26, 84, 89,
95; gatekeepers, 41, 69-70; importance
of, 20-21, 25, 36-37, 47, 51, 60, 62, 136;
invisible in, 116; joy in, 36; as lesson, 105,
113; marginalized vs. mainstream, 36-39,
136; memories and remembering, 16-17,
81, 83, 86-87, 90-94, 118, 121-124, 126-127,
144, 147, 163, 170n3; narrators, 22, 25,
95, 125; as national creation myth, 62,
116; official, 15, 25, 34, 46, 50-51, 62-63,
71-75, 126, 136-137, 142, 145, 148; oral, 10,
20, 51, 75, 84-85, 90, 141, 145; as ongoing
exchange, 94, 109, 113-114; ownership,
26; place in, 125-128, 139, 170n2;
politics of, 12, 40, 42, 45, 51, 71; primary
source, 141-142, 145; production of,
144, 170n1; protection of, 19, 48, 52, 67;
public, 15, 21, 25-26, 30, 35, 49, 50-51;
Reconstruction Period, 33; recording
of, 11-15, 26, 49, 78, 140, 148; recording
of on tape, 11, 15, 17, 87-89, 91, 108, 125;
recording of on video, 13, 16, 21, 125, 134;
repertoire of narratives, 74, 77, 95-96;
sacred, 46, 59, 61-62, 68-69; as scientific
research, 141, 144; as source of identity,
belonging, and pride, 62, 66, 164; and
social status, 37; subjects of, 22, 25, 137;
writing/making, 19-20, 22, 30, 36, 38-
39, 48, 51, 126, 138; written record, 75,
81, 125-126, 132-133, 140-141, 143, 169n3.
See also National Register of Historic
Places; Union: historic-ness of; Union:
history of

159; as suburb of Riverton, 54, 70; uniqueness/significance/specialness, 21, 25, 35, 51, 57, 59-60, 71, 154, 161, 164. *See also* National Register of Historic Places

Union Community Association (UCA), 2, 18-21, 26, 45, 48, 52, 59, 66-67, 133, 153, 164, 171n2; membership, 20, 23, 61, 66-67, 150, 171n2; person of the year, 19; picnic, 17-21, 23, 27, 32, 148, 149, 163

Union Historic District, 10, 20, 23, 40, 48, 50-58, 67-71, 118, 137, 154, 161, 163; historic recognition, 2, 7, 9-10, 19-22, 27, 30, 45-51, 60-67, 70, 74, 122, 133, 135, 137, 148-149, 156-157, 164, 169n2

Unveiling ceremony, 4, 26, 40, 46, 48-52, 57-59, 67, 150, 157; as rite of passage, 52-63

Virginia, 8, 9, 149; law, 63

Wade family, 130
white privilege, 118-119, 132
whiteness, 23, 33, 49; marginalization, 33, 34, 35, 138
work ethic, 105

ABOUT THE AUTHOR

Mieka Brand Polanco is Associate Professor of Anthropology at James Madison University. Polanco studies the complex relationship between human beings and their social and physical landscapes, especially as it bears on questions of race and racialization. Her research in African American anthropology centers on issues of space, race, and history.